A
bounty
OF bead
& wire
NECKLACES

A bounty OF bead & wire NECKLACES

50 fun, fast JEWELRY projects

NATHALIE MORNU

LARK CRAFTS

Asheville

Art Director
Carol Morse Barnao

Art Intern
Jessica Yee

Editorial Assistance
Abby Haffelt
Dawn Dillingham
Hannah Doyle

Cover Designer
Carol Morse Barnao

LARK CRAFTS

An Imprint of Sterling Publishing
387 Park Avenue South
New York, NY 10016

**If you have questions or comments about
this book, please visit: larkcrafts.com**

Library of Congress Cataloging-in-Publication Data

Mornu, Nathalie.
  A bounty of bead & wire necklaces : 50 fun, fast jewelry projects. -- 1st ed.
      p. cm.
  Author: Nathalie Mornu.
  Includes index.
  ISBN 978-1-4547-0289-4
  1. Jewelry making. 2. Necklaces. 3. Beadwork. 4. Wire jewelry. I. Title. II. Title: Bounty of bead and wire necklaces.
  TT212.M665 2012
  739.27--dc23
                                    2011037348
10 9 8 7 6 5 4 3 2 1

First Edition

Published by Lark Crafts
An Imprint of Sterling Publishing Co., Inc.
387 Park Avenue South, New York, NY 10016

© 2012, Lark Crafts, an Imprint of Sterling Publishing Co., Inc.

This book is comprised of materials from the following Lark Crafts and Sterling Publishing titles, with all text, photography,
and illustrations © Lark Crafts unless otherwise specified:
Beading with Charms © 2007
Beading with Filigree, text © 2008, Cynthia Deis
Beading with Gemstones, text © 2007, Valérie MacCarthy
Beading with Pearls © 2008
Beading with World Beads © 2009
Bead Love © 2006
Contemporary Bead & Wire Jewelry © 2006
Elegant Wire Jewelry, text © 2007, Kathleen Ann Frey
Beading with Crystals © 2007
Beading Vintage-Style Jewelry, text © 2007, Marty Stevens-Heebner and Christine Calla
French-Inspired Jewelry, text © 2007, Kaari Meng; photography & illustrations © 2007, Red Lips 4 Courage Communications, Inc.
Healing Jewelry © 2007, Prolific Impressions and Sterling Publishing
Dazzling Bead & Wire Crafts © 2005, Prolific Impressions and Sterling Publishing

Distributed in Canada by Sterling Publishing,
c/o Canadian Manda Group, 165 Dufferin Street
Toronto, Ontario, Canada M6K 3H6

Distributed in the United Kingdom by GMC Distribution Services,
Castle Place, 166 High Street, Lewes, East Sussex, England BN7 1XU

Distributed in Australia by Capricorn Link (Australia) Pty Ltd.,
P.O. Box 704, Windsor, NSW 2756 Australia

Manufactured in China

ISBN 13: 978-1-4547-0289-4

For information about custom editions, special sales, and premium and corporate purchases, please contact the Sterling Special Sales Department at
800-805-5489 or specialsales@sterlingpub.com.

Requests for information about desk and examination copies available to college and university professors must be submitted to
academic@larkbooks.com. Our complete policy can be found at www.larkcrafts.com.

contents

22

25

28

30

32

34

36

39

42

46

48

51

154

 118

 121

 124

 126

 128

 132

136

138

141

152

144

146

150

introduction

Think of your neck as a blank canvas just waiting for colors and textures—beads, charms, and chains—to adorn it. Whether it features an antique pendant, a wire-wrapped gemstone, or strands of pearls, each necklace in this book can reflect your own unique style, since you'll make it yourself! From French-inspired filigree to African trade beads, a bounty of choices awaits you.

Glance through the 50 fun, fast projects. Start with your favorite, or pick one according to your skill level. Challenge your wireworking skills with Vortex (page 48), featuring a large turquoise pendant set off by a chain crafted entirely from handmade links in spirals and waves. For an exotic twist, try your hand at Anemone (page 68), with its snaking cluster of snow jade beads wrapped with black, spiraled wire. Get more color in your life from Lucille (page 91), featuring an asymmetrical assemblage of brass filigree pinwheels and red glass beads hung on a sprawling brass chain. With this project, follow your instincts when arranging accent beads along the chain, giving it your personal creative flair.

Whether you've been beading for years or you can barely make a wire loop, *A Bounty of Bead & Wire Necklaces* offers something for every skill level. The projects include step-by-step instructions, photo illustrations, and designers' tips to spare you even a moment of confusion. And if you ever feel you're in too deep, just go back to the Basics section to refresh yourself on everything from making simple loops to sewing beads to filigree.

So stop daydreaming and start making! With a bounty of bead and wire necklaces to choose from, what's keeping you from handcrafting your favorite necklace today?

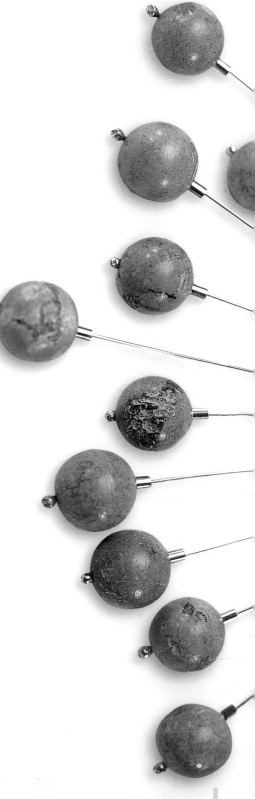

basics

An artist can easily picture wire as a linear element, and beads as dots or points. All of the projects in this book transform these simple building blocks into chic necklaces.

MATERIALS AND TOOLS

The basic materials and tools described here make up the essential jewelry-making kit, ready and waiting to be expanded upon. The real fun comes in when browsing for your beads and wire; it's a little like taking a trip around the globe: you'll find African trade beads, lampworked glass crafted in India, cloisonné treasures made in China, shimmering Austrian crystal, and wire from, well, all over.

Beads

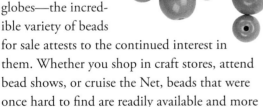

Elegant pearls, faceted gem briolettes, Bali beads, glass donuts, drilled pebbles, resin globes—the incredible variety of beads for sale attests to the continued interest in them. Whether you shop in craft stores, attend bead shows, or cruise the Net, beads that were once hard to find are readily available and more affordable than ever.

If you've never worked in this medium, you're in for some fun hours of bead browsing— the hardest part is stopping! Most beads are organized in stores by their material, shape, and diameter.

Sizing

Beads are measured in millimeters. If you're more accustomed to inches, the comparison chart will help you as you shop (figure 1). You can buy beads individually or in strands. Most strands are 16 inches (40.6 cm) long, with the number of beads on each strand determined by individual size.

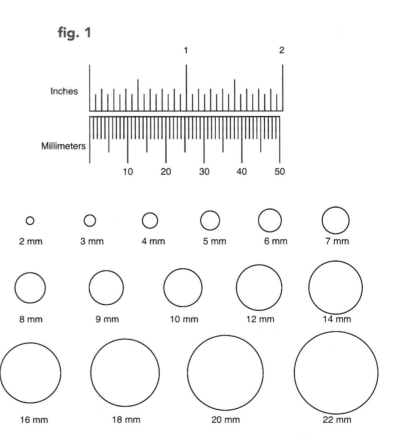

fig. 1

Holes: Orientation and Diameter

Some beads need to be tested for fit on the wire or findings of choice. The position and size of the hole, or drill, in the bead, crystal, or pearl will have a huge effect on the finished piece because it determines how the object will be attached.

A bead with a hole that runs from the top to the bottom is called length drilled. This is the most common treatment. You can assume that supply lists are calling for length-drilled beads if nothing is specified. When the hole is through the width, it's a horizontal drill. As the name implies, a top-drilled bead, crystal, or pearl has a hole near the top.

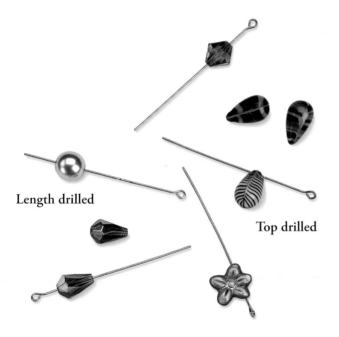

Length drilled

Top drilled

The size of a hole is another concern. Some beads may need larger holes if your project requires stronger, thicker wire. Some suppliers might let you request a strand that includes beads with larger holes. Depending on the product, the hole size may not be consistent from one bead to the next.

Wire

Traditionally, wire made from sterling silver or gold has been a popular choice for bead and wire jewelry, but many other wire products may be used, too. Metal craft wire is now available in a wide variety of colors; relative newcomers include anodized and dyed metals, such as aluminum, or niobium. Still other kinds of wire include steel, brass, nickel, copper, and even platinum. Finally, unlike these more malleable metals, super-springy memory wire, made from base metal or stainless steel, can be stretched and permanently bent, but it will always retain its initial coiled silhouette.

Various gauges and types of wire (from top): gold wire, silver wire, and memory wire

Whatever the metal, most wire comes in a large range of sizes and shapes, or profiles. Gauge is a scale of measurement that indicates a wire's diameter—the higher the numeral, the finer the wire. (Memory wire is the exception to gauge measurements; it's sold in sizes to fit the neck, wrist, or finger.) The Key to Wire Gauges chart below lists some helpful information about wire gauges and their specifications, both metric and standard.

key to wire gauges

AWG IN.	AWG MM	GAUGE	SWG IN.	SWG MM
0.204	5.18	4	0.232	5.89
0.182	4.62	5	0.212	5.38
0.162	4.12	6	0.192	4.88
0.144	3.66	7	0.176	4.47
0.129	3.28	8	0.160	4.06
0.114	2.90	9	0.144	3.66
0.102	2.59	10	0.128	3.25
0.091	2.31	11	0.116	2.95
0.081	2.06	12	0.104	2.64
0.072	1.83	13	0.092	2.34
0.064	1.63	14	0.080	2.03
0.057	1.45	15	0.072	1.83
0.051	1.30	16	0.064	1.63
0.045	1.14	17	0.056	1.42
0.040	1.02	18	0.048	1.22
0.036	0.914	19	0.040	1.02
0.032	0.813	20	0.036	0.914
0.029	0.737	21	0.032	0.813
0.025	0.635	22	0.028	0.711
0.023	0.584	23	0.024	0.610
0.020	0.508	24	0.022	0.559
0.018	0.457	25	0.020	0.508
0.016	0.406	26	0.018	0.457

Using gauges other than those specified in the instructions is fine, but keep in mind that very thin wire, though easier to shape, isn't strong enough for a lot of heavy beads, and very thick wire isn't suitable for small-scale designs—not to mention the limitation of the size of a bead's hole. Wires of the same gauge will all feel a bit different to manipulate because some metals are softer than others. However, wire stiffens a bit as you work with it, adding more support to your work. This process is called work hardening. If wire gets handled too much, it becomes brittle and breaks.

Silver and gold wires are made and sold in different hardnesses: dead soft, soft, and half hard. In most cases, our designers have recommended the appropriate silver or gold wire hardness for their projects; when in doubt, use half-hard wire. Avoid dead-soft wire; it's difficult to work with and won't retain shaping or angles.

Many of the projects use sterling silver wire, but wire made from an alloy—a blend of less expensive metals—is an acceptable substitute, especially for jewelry for everyday wear. It's a great idea to use an inexpensive practice wire of a similar gauge and hardness if you plan to make a piece of jewelry from very expensive wire.

Depending on the metal, wire is sold many different ways: on spools, in prepackaged coils, by weight, and by length. Look for various types in jewelry supply shops, craft retailers, and certain areas of hardware stores, including the electrical supply and framing departments. The Internet is also a vast resource for wire of every kind.

Findings

In beading, you'll often need more than just beads and wire to create your final piece. Findings are that extra ingredient. They're usually made of metal and are meant to connect, finish, and embellish your jewelry designs.

Bead caps fit over the tops and bottoms of beads. They're used to finish a strand of beads or as spacers between beads.

Chain is made up of connected loops of wire. The loops can come in several forms, including round, oval, twisted, and hammered.

Clasps connect wire ends to hold the necklace closed. There are dozens of different types. Here are some of the most common.

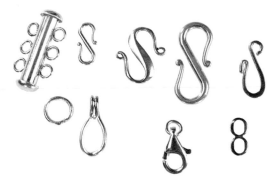

Box clasps have one half that's comprised of a hollow box. The other half is a tab that clicks into the box to lock the clasp.

Hook-and-eye clasps have one half that's shaped like a hook, the other half like a loop, or an "eye." The hook passes through the eye to secure the clasp.

Lobster clasps are spring-activated clasps that are shaped like their name.

Magnetic clasps use powerful magnets to make the connection between one half of the clasp and the other. Use these only with fairly lightweight pieces, and if you have a pacemaker, don't use them at all.

Toggle clasps have one half that looks like a ring with a loop attached to it, and the other half looks like a bar. Pass the bar through the ring, and once the bar lies parallel on top of the ring, you've secured the clasp.

Connectors allow you to make the transition from one beaded strand to many strands.

Crimp tubes and crimp beads secure the ends of beading wire to keep the beads on while providing means for attaching a clasp or finding.

Eye pins are straight pieces of wire with a simple loop at one end. They're used to make beaded links.

Head pins are used for stringing beads to make dangles. Simple head pins are composed of a straight wire with a tiny disk at one end to hold beads in place. Ball-end head pins have a ball at the end instead of a disk. There are even fancier head pins, too.

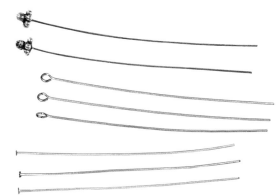

Jump rings are circular loops of wire used to connect beadwork to findings or findings to findings. They come in open and soldered-closed versions. You can find them at any beading or craft retail store in a variety of colors and metals.

Spacers are small elements used to separate and set off the beads in a design. They can be plain or fancy.

Basic Tools

Making bead and wire jewelry requires surprisingly few tools, and all are pretty low tech. As with other jewelry-making materials, be sure to buy the best type you can afford.

Pliers have either serrated or smooth surfaces on their jaws. If you're going to invest in a set of pliers, make sure they're smooth jawed. These are preferable for jewelry making because they won't scratch wire. If you want to use the serrated pliers you already have, you can wrap the jaws with surgical adhesive tape to protect your work—just be careful to avoid getting any of the adhesive on your materials.

Chain-nose pliers feature jaws that are flat on the inside but taper to a point on the outside. This type of pliers also comes in a bent version used for grasping hard-to-reach places.

Crimping pliers attach crimp beads and crimp tubes to beading wire. See page 19 for instructions on how to use these.

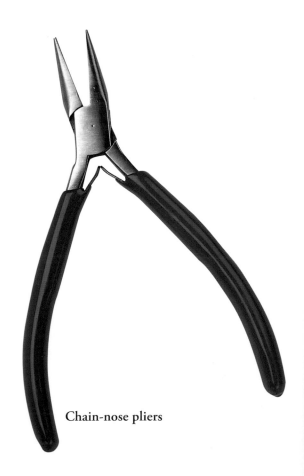

Chain-nose pliers

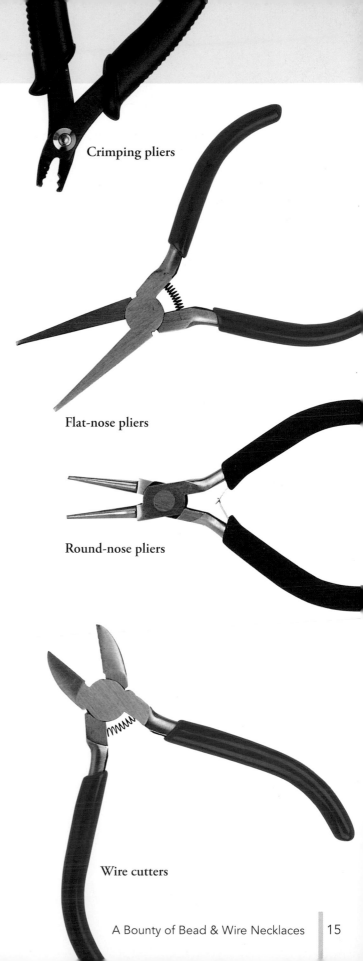

Flat-nose pliers have jaws that are flat on the inside and have a square nose.

Round-nose pliers have cylindrical jaws that taper to a very fine point.

Wire cutters have very sharp blades that come to a point. One side of the pliers leaves a V-shaped cut; the other side leaves a flat, or flush, cut.

Jigs are made up of a flat board with pegs. The pegs are placed at desired intervals to help bend wire into perfect loops. You can purchase them commercially or easily make your own.

Mandrels are any straight or tapered rod around which you can wrap wire to shape it into coils. It's an essential tool for making jump rings, the loops in closures, or uniformly sized units for links. You can buy one with various diameters (shown here) or simply use a nail, knitting needle, dowel, or any household item with a rodlike shape.

Crimping pliers

Flat-nose pliers

Round-nose pliers

Wire cutters

Knitting needles

Mandrel

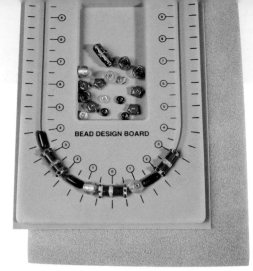

Bead board

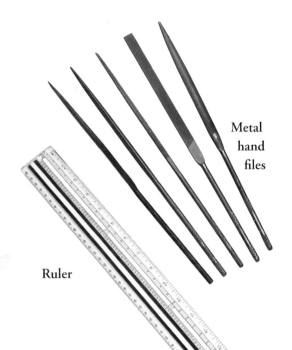

Metal hand files

Ruler

Emery boards are used in these projects for sanding wire smooth.

Metal hand files, or needle files, have very fine teeth. They also smooth wire ends.

Tape measures and rulers are used in this book to determine where to cut wire and chain. They're also helpful for checking jewelry lengths and bead and finding sizes. Choose one that has both standard and metric markings.

Bead boards allow you to organize and lay out beads for your design, while helping you measure length with precision. They're inexpensive but not indispensable. In a pinch, you can lay your beads out on a towel to prevent them from rolling as you work.

Safety glasses are important to wear when making metal jewelry. They protect your eyes from flying wire pieces.

TECHNIQUES

A wide variety of skills is required to make all the projects in this book, but have no fear. By studying the techniques below, you'll be working like a pro in no time.

Wireworking

Now for the fun: learning how to wrangle wire into a great necklace design using basic wire techniques. Unless you're already familiar with them, you'll probably want to practice these techniques with a low-cost wire first—it's not easy to straighten wire once it's bent the wrong way. The results might be good enough to use for a later project.

Wire Control

To keep spooled wire under control, put it in a small plastic storage bag. Pull out a length of wire as needed. If you're working with a coil of wire rather than a spool, wrap a piece of masking tape around it so it can't spring open in all directions. Good-looking jewelry pieces are those with smooth and confident swoops, angles, and curves, made from kink-free wire.

Straightening

To keep it in good condition, wire is stored and sold in coils. Coiling wire saves space, but it's best to straighten out its curve before you begin working with it. To straighten a short length of wire,

Safety glasses

hold one end of it with chain-nose pliers. Just above the pliers, grasp the wire with a cloth or paper towel to keep your hands clean and to prevent friction burn. Squeezing your fingers slightly, pull the length of wire through them.

If the wire bends or crimps at any time, gently run your finger along it to smooth the kink, or rub the wire over the edge of a table padded with newspaper. Don't smooth a crimp too vigorously, or the wire could break. Remember, the more you shape the wire, the more it work hardens and becomes brittle.

Coiling

Coiling, or tightly wrapping, wire is primarily used in this book for attaching one wire to another and creating decorative coils. Start by grasping the base—a thick wire, dowel, or knitting needle—tightly in one hand. Hold the wrapping wire with your other hand and make one wrap. Reposition your hands so you can continue to wrap the wire around the base wire, making tight revolutions (photo 1).

Spiraling

Spiraling is a great technique to add depth and embellishment to your design, or even to create the focal point of your piece.

1. Use the tip of a pair of round-nose pliers to curve one end of the wire into a half-circle or hook shape about ⅛ inch (3 mm) in diameter (see figure 2).

2. Use the very tips of the pliers to curve the end of the wire tightly into itself, as shown in figure 3, aiming to keep the shape round rather than oval. Hold the spiral in flat- or chain-nose pliers and push the loose end of the wire against the already-coiled form (see figure 4); as you continue, reposition the wire in the pliers as needed.

Making Simple Loops

1. Use chain-nose pliers to make a 90° bend ⅜ inch (1 cm) from the end of the wire; or if you're using the loop to secure a bead (as with a bead dangle), make the 90° bend right at the top of the bead, then cut the wire ⅜ inch (1 cm) from the top of the bead (photo 2).

2. Use round-nose pliers to grasp the wire end and roll the pliers until the wire touches the 90° bend (photo 3).

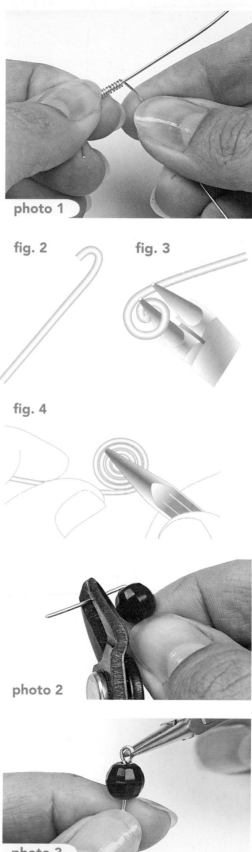

photo 1

fig. 2   fig. 3

fig. 4

photo 2

photo 3

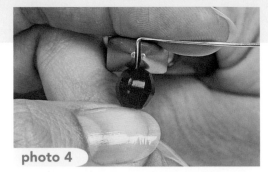

photo 4

photo 5

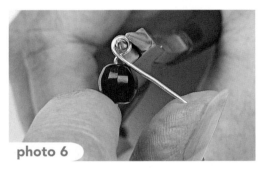

photo 6

photo 7

photo 8

Making Wrapped Loops

1. Use chain-nose pliers to make a 90° bend in the wire 2 inches (5.1 cm) from one wire end or ¼ inch (6 mm) from the top of a bead (photo 4).

2. Using round-nose pliers to grasp the bend, shape the wire over the top jaw (photo 5), and swing it underneath to form a partial loop (photo 6).

3. Use chain-nose pliers or your fingers to wrap the wire in a tight coil down the stem (photo 7). Then trim the excess wire close to the wrap and use chain-nose pliers to tighten the wire end.

Note: You may notice that some project instructions say to bend the wire 45°, rather than 90°. This bend keeps the loop centered above the bead and prevents it from veering to one side just as well as the 90° bend does (photo 8).

Making Triangular Wraps

This wrap looks great on a bead that is drilled through the width or top drilled, or a bicone you want to position horizontally.

1. Cut a piece of wire 2 inches (5.1 cm) long. With flat-nose pliers, bend the last ½ inch (1.3 cm) of the wire upward. Thread a bead onto the wire.

2. Fold up the other side of the wire until the pieces cross directly above the bead, creating a hat (figure 5).

3. Take the chain-nose pliers to the base of the longer wire, and bend it back down a bit. Use the round-nose pliers to make a simple loop (figure 6).

4. Finish the piece by wrapping the end of the longer wire around the base several times. Snip off the excess wire and file the end, or else tuck it underneath the last loop.

When attaching these beads, make sure the direction of the loop brings attention to the bead instead of the wire. If you've already completed your loop and it is not facing the direction you prefer, simply grip the loop with round-nose pliers and give it a small additional twist to make the loop either forward facing or side facing, whichever is needed for your piece. Following up with this small but important detail will allow the bead to be the focus of your design.

Using a Jig

Jigs are especially handy because they allow you to quickly create multiple wire designs, all of them identical. A jig is basically a flat surface with equidistant holes. You place pegs in these holes to form the desired pattern, and then you wrap wire around them to form a looped wire design (photo 9). Be sure to experiment with inexpensive wire until you're pleased with the results of your jig work, then switch to precious-metal wire to make your jewelry design.

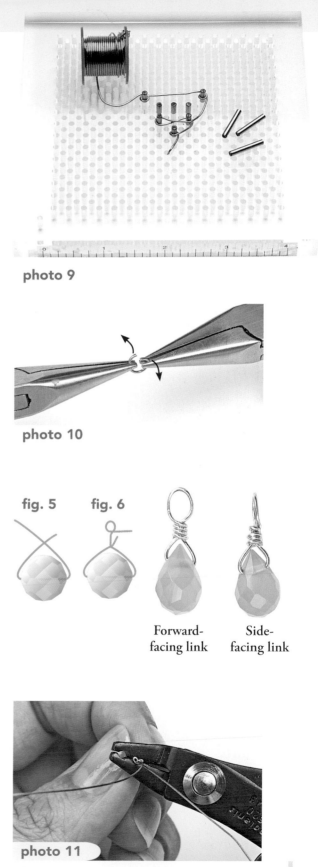

photo 9

Finishing Off Wires

When you're done with a piece of wire, clip the tails, and press them down so there will be no sharp ends sticking out of your finished piece that could scratch or stab you or snag your clothes. Then run your fingers across the area to check for sharp ends. If you find some, keep pressing them down and/or clip them a bit more. If necessary, file the tip of the wire with an emery board or a hand file.

photo 10

Stringing

Stringing beads is a simple act—simply pass wire through a bead, and you've got it! It's how you arrange beads on the stringing material that creates masterpieces—that's what takes practice.

Opening and Closing Jump Rings

Always open a jump ring with two pairs of pliers, one positioned on each side of the split. Push one pair of pliers away from you, and pull the other one toward you (photo 10). This way the ring will be opened laterally, instead of horizontally, which can weaken the wire. You'll want to open any other wire loop you work with the same way.

fig. 5 **fig. 6**

Forward-facing link

Side-facing link

Crimping

Crimping is a technique used to attach wire to a finding.

1. String one crimp bead and then the finding. Pass the wire end back through the crimp bead in the opposite direction.

2. Next, slide the crimp bead against the finding so it's snug, but not so tight that the wire can't move freely. Squeeze the crimp bead in the U-shaped notch—the notch furthest from the tip—of the crimping pliers (photo 11).

3. Rotate the crimp bead and nestle it into the front notch. Gently squeeze the bead so it collapses on itself into a nicely shaped tube (photo 12; see next page).

photo 11

photo 12

photo 13

Sewing Beads to Filigree

Flexible beading wire is the best option when attaching beads to filigree—the wire knots easily and won't damage your fingers. Always try to match the color of the wire to the filigree. This will ensure that any exposed sewing wire blends in and isn't noticed, much like matching your thread when sewing on a button! This technique can create a mess on the back of the filigree with the knots and tail strands everywhere, so you may want to add another piece of filigree to the back side of your design.

1. Cut the required amount of beading wire, and string on one bead, leaving a 4-inch (10.2-cm) tail. Working from the front of the filigree, push both ends of the wire through the filigree holes where specified in the instructions (photo 13).

fig. 7

2. Tie a secure square knot on the back of the filigree (photo 14). A square knot (figure 7) is made by forming an overhand knot with both ends of the stringing material, right end over left end. Repeat this, passing the left end over the right end to make the knot tight and secure.

photo 14

3. Pass the long end of the wire up through the filigree to exit where specified (photo 15). Slip on a bead and pass the wire down through the filigree to the back side.

4. Repeat this sewing action until the filigree is beaded as required (photo 16). Tie the wire ends together in a tight square knot and trim. If you are worried about your knots holding, you can add a drop of glue, but it is usually unnecessary.

Working with Chain

Chain is one of the simplest materials to use in jewelry making. The toughest part is deciding which type to use! After that, all you need to do is cut the chain and create your piece.

The lengths of chain you'll need for the projects are specified in each set of directions. Rulers are helpful, but you shouldn't always rely on them for determining the length of chain to cut. Instead, when working with multiple pieces of chain that are supposed to be the same length, count links. The difference of even one small chain link will make your earrings noticeably lopsided. Use a ruler to measure just the first length of chain, then count the links in that segment, and count all additional chain segments to make absolutely certain that each one has exactly the same number of links. After

photo 15

photo 16

you determine the right length for the piece you're making, pull out your trusty wire cutters and snip away.

To attach a chain to wire or a finding, slide one link of the chain (often an end link) onto a wire loop or finding. Generally, the chain is secured with wrapped wire.

Polishing

You can polish your jewelry with a jewelry buffing cloth—sometimes called a rouge cloth—or papers, which are available from most jewelry suppliers. Before using any cleaning solution, test it on a scrap piece of wire first. A tumbler is an option for some pieces, but make sure you're familiar with its operation and consider that many beads aren't suitable for the process.

Take Time to Plan

One of the hardest steps in beading is making yourself take the time to develop a plan. Who can blame you? When faced with an array of beautiful beads, all you want to do is get to work. However, just think of planning as more fun time you can spend with your beads. Use a bead board (page 16) or lay them out on a towel so they won't roll around. Place different types and colors of spacer beads between the larger beads. Experiment with some common designs, as shown in figure 8, and arrange and rearrange to your heart's content until you have a design you can't live without.

Length

Do you want your necklace to be a demure choker, a pretty princess, or a dramatic rope? Different lengths, shown in figure 9, go by different names. What lengths are you willing to go to?

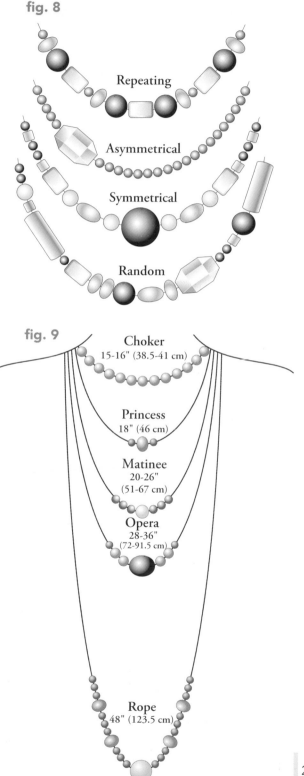

fig. 8

Repeating

Asymmetrical

Symmetrical

Random

fig. 9

Choker
15-16" (38.5-41 cm)

Princess
18" (46 cm)

Matinee
20-26"
(51-67 cm)

Opera
28-36"
(72-91.5 cm)

Rope
48" (123.5 cm)

grapevine

For a special night out, embellish yourself with this dramatic necklace featuring large amethyst focal beads.

Designer: Valérie MacCarthy

Finished size: 15½ inches (39.4 cm);
    longer dangle, 4 inches (10.2 cm)

Materials

2 extra-large amethyst drops, 40 mm

3 amethyst nuggets, 20 mm

4 amethyst beads, 10 mm

2 sterling silver beads, 3 mm

2 sterling silver ball-end head pins,
    2½ inches (6.4 cm) long

1 sterling silver lobster clasp

48-inch (122 cm) length of 1.5-mm
    sterling silver chain

15-inch (38.1 cm) length of 24-gauge
    sterling silver wire

Tools

Chain-nose pliers

Round-nose pliers

Wire cutters

Large rubberized round-nose pliers

Ruler

Instructions

1. Slide one 3-mm silver bead and one large 40-mm amethyst drop onto a 2½-inch (6.4 cm) ball-end head pin.

2. Bend the top of the ball-end pin 45°. Hold the pin with the round-nose pliers and bend the pin around the pliers. Place this loop onto the first link of the silver chain. Using the chain-nose pliers, hold the loop and twist the wire to secure the silver bead, the amethyst drop, and the silver chain link.

3. Cut the chain, leaving a ½-inch (1.3 cm) length attached.

4. Repeat steps 1 and 2 with the second 40-mm amethyst drop, this time measuring and cutting the silver chain to leave a 2-inch (5.1 cm) length attached.

5. With the 24-gauge wire, use the round-nose pliers to make a loop about ¾ inch (1.9 cm) from the end. Place both chain ends attached to the two large amethyst drops onto this loop. Hold the loop with the chain-nose pliers and twist to secure. Cut off the shorter wire end.

6. Slide the 24-gauge wire through one 20-mm amethyst nugget. Bend the wire at the top about 45°. Using the round-nose pliers, bend the wire around to secure.

7. Cut the chain to make six segments in the following lengths: two short segments each 1½ inches (3.8 cm), two medium segments each 1¾ inches (4.4 cm), and two long segments each 2 inches (5.1 cm). (**Note:** Count the links before cutting the chain to make sure that each pair of chain segments is exactly the same.)

8. Place the six chain segments onto the looped wire in the following order: long, medium, short, short, medium, long.

Designer's Tip

When working with multiple chains that are attached together, make sure the chains don't tangle or twist by keeping all of the chain links facing the same direction. Let the chains hang while working with them so you'll be able to see each chain. Careful attention to the details makes a big difference in the overall appearance of fine jewelry.

9. After all of the chain segments are in place on the wire loop, hold the loop with the chain-nose pliers and wrap the wire around to secure all pieces in place.

10. Cut twelve ¾-inch (1.9 cm) chain segments. This is worth repeating: Count the links before cutting to make sure all of them are exactly the same length.

11. Make a new wire loop using the round-nose pliers. Select three consecutive chains from one side, choosing one of each length: long, medium, and short. Place the three chains onto the loop.

12. Hold this loop with the chain-nose pliers and twist the wire around to secure. Cut off the shorter wire end.

13. Slide one 10-mm amethyst bead onto the wire (figure 1). Bend the wire 45°, hold it with the round-nose pliers, and loop it around.

14. Place three ¾-inch (1.9 cm) chain segments onto the loop. Hold the loop with the chain-nose pliers and wrap the wire around to secure. Cut off the excess wire.

15. Make a new loop in the wire with the round-nose pliers. Place all three ends of the ¾-inch (1.9 cm) chain segments onto the loop. Using the chain-nose pliers, twist the wire around to secure. Cut off the shorter wire end.

16. Slide a 20-mm amethyst nugget onto the wire. Bend the wire 45° and use the round-nose pliers to loop it. Place three ¾-inch (1.9 cm) chain segments onto the loop and use the chain-nose pliers to wrap the wire to secure. Cut off the excess wire.

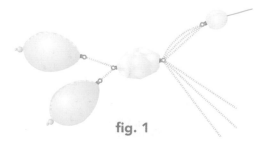

fig. 1

17. Make a new loop in the wire using the round-nose pliers. Place three ¾-inch (1.9 cm) chain segments onto the loop and twist the wires around to secure. Cut off the shorter wire end.

18. Place another 10-mm amethyst bead onto this wire. Bend the wire 45° and use the round-nose pliers to loop the wire around to secure.

19. Cut six 3-inch (7.6 cm) chain segments. Place three of them onto the loop you've just made. Hold the loop with the chain-nose pliers and wrap the wire around to secure. Cut off the excess wire.

20. Pick up the three remaining chain segments (one each of short, medium, and long) from step 11. Repeat steps 11 through 19 to make the other side of the necklace.

21. You're now ready to attach the lobster clasp to the back of the necklace. Using the 24-gauge wire and round-nose pliers, make a new loop. Place the three chains from one side of the necklace onto this loop. Hold the loop with the chain-nose pliers and twist the wires to secure them. Cut off the shorter wire end.

22. Bend the wire 45° and loop it again with the round-nose pliers. Slide the lobster clasp onto this loop and hold the loop with the chain-nose pliers. Wrap the wire around the twist you made in step 21 and cut off the excess wire.

23. On the other side of the necklace, make the hook for the clasp. Make a new loop in the wire. Place all three chains onto this loop and twist the wires to secure. Cut off the shorter wire end.

24. Grip the wire with the rubberized round-nose pliers and loop it around. Then hold the loop with these pliers and wrap the wire around the twist you made in step 23. Cut off the excess wire.

bewitched

Create your own shapes to make enchanting charms. Mix and match your choices to make a one-of-a-kind necklace that will bewitch everyone.

bewitched

Designer: Kathy Frey

Finished size: 18 inches (45.7 cm) long

Materials

26-inch (66 cm) length of 22-gauge half-hard sterling silver wire

3-foot (91 cm) length of 26-gauge sterling silver wire

18-inch (45.7 cm) length of sterling silver chain with clasp

32 semiprecious stone, glass, or pearl beads to fit on 26-gauge wire, 2 to 3 mm

Tools

Wire cutters

Chain-nose pliers

Round-nose pliers

Fine-point permanent marker

Planishing hammer

Steel block

Burnisher

Liver of sulfur (optional)

Designer's Tip

You can change the look of this piece greatly by using 20-gauge wire instead of 22-gauge wire for the frames. If you're working with the heavier gauge, in step 5 you only need to tap the curves in the frame rather than hammering the whole shape to add strength.

Instructions

1. To make the triangular frame, use wire cutters to flush trim the tips of the 22-gauge wire. Use chain-nose pliers to form a bend in the wire, 2½ to 3 inches (6.4 to 7.6 cm) from the end. Fold the wire ends toward each other to form the point of a long, thin triangle.

2. Use chain-nose pliers to bend the corners of the triangle about 1 to 1½ inches (2.5 to 3.8 cm) up from the point. Make these bends so they are at sharp angles to each other (photo 1).

3. Use chain-nose pliers to form a post by bending the short tail at a 90° angle from the center top side (photo 2). Bend the long tail at the angle just made. Coil the long tail around the post twice (photo 3). Use wire cutters to flush cut the long tail and use chain-nose pliers to tuck it in.

4. Use chain-nose pliers to bend the exposed post wire at a 90° angle directly on top of the coil. Use wire cutters to flush cut the wire to a loop length and round-nose pliers to form a simple loop. Make sure the loop is facing the right way for the shape to lie flat when it dangles from the chain.

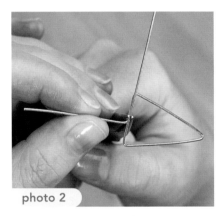
photo 2

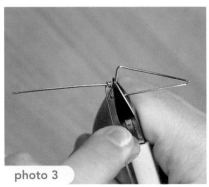
photo 3

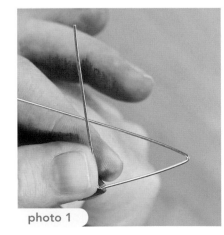
photo 1

26

5. To add strength, use a planishing hammer and steel block to gently hammer the entire shape. Do not flatten it.

6. To make the other four wire charms, you can either sketch shapes for templates or work free-form. Using the 22-gauge wire in lengths of 1 to 2 inches (2.5 to 5.1 cm), create organic, curvy shapes that contrast geometric forms and vary in length.

7. Apply any desired finishes to the frames. ***Note:*** If you wish to darken your piece, oxidize all of the frames, as well as the wrapping wire and the chain before moving on to the next steps.

8. To wrap the shapes, use chain-nose pliers to tightly coil the end of the 26-gauge wire twice around one top side of one of the shapes. Use wire cutters to flush cut the short tail and chain-nose pliers to tuck in the tail so it sits neatly inside the frame.

Gently pull the wire across to the other side of the frame. ***Note:*** The closed, flat shapes can be awkward to stop and start. Just remember that you are in control and place the wire where you want it.

9. Thread one or two beads onto the wrapping wire, pull the wire across the frame, and wrap it once around the other side. These side wraps should be tight but not so closely spaced that the beads can't slide around.

10. Continue wrapping and adding beads as you work toward the bottom tip. You'll need to hold the wraps in place and be careful not to pull too tightly, or the wires will slide down the form.

11. When you reach the tip, end by coiling the wire twice around the frame. Use wire cutters to flush cut the wire and chain-nose pliers to tuck in the tail so that it sits neatly inside the frame.

12. Use chain-nose pliers to add kinks to the wires and to position the beads where you want them, leaving enough space for the beads to slide.

13. To finish the necklace, use flat-nose pliers to open the loop on the charm that you'd like to place at the middle of the chain, just as you would a jump ring. Attach the loop to the middle link on the chain and then close the loop. Continue adding charms in this manner, working from the center outward. Count the links between charms to achieve even spacing.

globetrotter

This fresh and spontaneous necklace has been carefully arranged to make sure the beads take center stage.

Designer: Joanna Gollberg

Finished size: Longest dangle, 4 inches (10.3 cm)

Materials

11 turquoise beads, 12 mm

11 sterling silver head pins

43 tube crimp beads, 4 x 3 mm

Sterling silver hard neck wire

Tools

Wire cutters

Round-nose pliers

Instructions

1. Trim the head pins to varying lengths from 1 to 4 inches (2.5 to 10.3 cm) long. String a 12-mm bead on each head pin, followed by one tube crimp bead.

2. Arrange the beaded dangles in their stringing order, making sure that no beads touch. You want the pattern to look random. When you're satisfied with the layout, snip off any extra length from the head pins as needed.

3. Make a loop on the end of each head pin. To prevent the dangle from falling off the neck wire, make sure each loop is a complete closed circle.

4. String one crimp bead on the neck wire, followed by one dangle, followed by three more crimp beads. Continue alternating one dangle with three crimp beads until the last dangle is on the wire. Then string on one more crimp bead to complete the necklace.

transformation

Snowflake obsidian rondelles
and a disc are combined with
onyx beads and sections of silver
chain. A silver butterfly charm,
a symbol of transformation,
is suspended from the disc.

Materials

Designer: Patty Cox

Finished size: 26 inches (66 cm)

100 (approx.) snowflake obsidian rondelles, 6mm

1 snowflake obsidian disc, 35 mm

7 round black onyx beads, 8 mm

8 round black onyx beads, 3 mm

26 inches (66 cm) of silver-plated figaro chain, 2.3 mm

1 silver-plated lobster clasp

10 silver eye pins

40 (approx.) silver jump rings, 4 mm

1 silver butterfly charm

2 silver crimp beads

Beading wire, .015

Tools

Wire cutters

Crimping tool

Round-nose pliers

Ruler

Instructions

1. To make the beaded eye pins, thread two snowflake obsidian rondelles, an 8-mm onyx bead, and two snowflake obsidian rondelles onto an eye pin. Cut the wire ⅜ inch (1 cm) from the last bead. Form a loop in the wire end using round-nose pliers. Repeat the process to make six in all.

2. On an eye pin, thread a 3-mm black onyx bead, five snowflake obsidian rondelles, and a 3-mm black onyx bead. Cut the wire ⅜ inch (1 cm) from the last bead. Form a loop in the wire end using round-nose pliers. Repeat the process to make four in all.

3. To make the center of the outer strand, cut a 2-inch (5.1 cm) length of chain, and wrap it through the disc. Secure it snugly against the disc with a jump ring, allowing the end of the chain to fall below the disc.

4. Attach the butterfly charm to the end of the chain with a jump ring.

5. Cut a 2-inch (5.1 cm) length of chain, and wrap it through the top of the disc to make a loop for hanging. Secure the chain snugly around the disc with a jump ring. Cut the excess chain from around the jump ring.

6. Cut another 2-inch (5.1 cm) chain length, and attach the jump ring on the hanging loop to its center to make the necklace center.

7. To make the center of the inner strand, cut a 10-inch (25.4 cm) length of bead stringing wire. Thread a crimp bead on one wire end. Run the wire end back through the crimp bead, forming a ⅛-inch (3 mm) loop. Crimp the bead.

8. Thread 19 snowflake obsidian rondelle beads on the wire. Add an 8-mm black onyx bead and 19 snowflake obsidian rondelle beads.

9. Thread a crimp bead on the wire end. Thread the wire tail back through the crimp bead and several rondelle beads. Pull wires taut. Crimp the bead, and cut wire tail.

10. To assemble the outer strand, cut a 2-inch (5.1 cm) chain piece, and attach one of the beaded eye pins to it with a jump ring. You'll have ten in all—six for the outer strand and four for the inner strand. Set aside four of these.

11. On each end of the outer strand center 2-inch (5.1 cm) chain, working from the center to the end, attach in this order using jump rings: a beaded eye pin with 8-mm onyx and a 2-inch (5.1 cm) chain, a beaded eye pin with 5 rondelles and a 2-inch (5.1 cm) chain, a beaded eye pin with 8-mm onyx and a 2-inch (5.1 cm) chain.

12. To assemble the inner strand and finish the necklace, attach a 2-inch (5.1 cm) chain, a beaded eye pin with 8-mm onyx and a 2-inch (5.1 cm) chain, and a beaded eye pin with 5 rondelles on each end of the inner strand center.

13. Bring the necklace strands together on each side. Attach one end of each strand to one side of the clasp with a jump ring.

14. Attach the remaining ends to the other side of the clasp with a jump ring.

jackie

This French-inspired
piece features glass
pearls of varying sizes
and colors accented
with a pretty silk ribbon.

Designer: Kaari Meng

Finished size: 14 1/16 inches (35.7 cm) long

Materials

27 copper eye pins, 1 inch (2.5 cm) long

2 copper jump rings, 5 mm

1 ivory glass pearl, 20 mm

8 grey glass pearls, 7 mm

9 silver glass pearls, 9 mm

6 ivory glass pearls, 11 mm

3 smoke glass pearls, 15 mm

32-inch (81.3 cm) length of grey striped silk ribbon, ½ inch (1.3 cm) wide

Tools

Needle-nose pliers

Instructions

1. Thread each pearl onto an eye pin. Link all the pearls together into a chain by making basic loop links with the eye pins. You can link the pearls together in any order that is pleasing to you, or in the following sequence:

   - 15 mm
   - 9 mm
   - 7 mm
   - 11 mm
   - 9 mm
   - 7 mm
   - 11 mm
   - 9 mm
   - 9 mm
   - 7 mm
   - 15 mm
   - 9 mm
   - 7 mm
   - 11 mm
   - 9 mm
   - 15 mm
   - 7 mm
   - 9 mm
   - 11 mm
   - 7 mm
   - 20 mm
   - 9 mm
   - 7 mm
   - 11 mm
   - 9 mm
   - 7 mm
   - 11 mm

2. To finish the necklace, attach a 5-mm jump ring at each end of the strand. Thread the ribbon through the jump rings. *Note:* The piece can be adjusted to fit as a necklace or a double-wrapped bracelet.

fiesta

The energetic color combination of this necklace gives the impression you're wearing a party!

Materials

Designer: Kate Drew-Wilkinson

Finished size: 25½ inches (64.8 cm)

22 red ceramic donut beads,
½ inch (1.3 cm)

27 turquoise round ceramic beads,
8 mm

57 antique copper heishi spacer
beads

54 sterling silver round beads,
2.5 mm

6-foot (1.8 m) length of 20-gauge
half-hard silver wire

4 silver ball-end head pins,
2 inches (5.1 cm)

1 pierced silver pendant, 3.5 x 4.5 cm

1 silver S-clasp

Tools

Chain-nose pliers

2 pairs of round-nose pliers

Wire cutters

Ruler or tape measure

Instructions

1. Set aside seven donut beads, 11 round ceramic beads, 19 spacers, and 20 sterling silver beads.

2. Cut the wire into 3-inch (7.6 cm) pieces. Using one piece of wire, make a wrapped bead loop link with a sterling silver bead, a spacer, a round ceramic bead, another spacer, and another sterling silver bead on it. Slip a donut on a loop before closing it. Keep the loops large enough to allow the donut free movement.

3. Make another wrapped bead loop link threaded with the same beads as in step 2, slipping the donut from the previous link onto one loop and adding another donut to the loop at the other end. Repeat the process until you've used all the beads except those set aside in step 1. Slip the ends of the S-clasp onto the free loops at the beginning and end of the strand, closing the necklace.

4. Using the beads set aside in step 1, make a bead loop link threaded with the same beads as in step 2. Before closing the second loop, attach it to the sixth donut from the clasp. Repeat, attaching a bead loop link to the next four donuts. Make and attach two more bead loop links on the eighth donut.

5. Make a bead loop link threaded with a sterling silver bead, a spacer, and another sterling silver bead, adding the silver pendant to one loop; attach the other loop to the center link hanging on the eighth donut.

6. Thread a turquoise bead, a spacer, and a sterling silver bead on each ball-end head pin. Attach one each to the fifth and eleventh donuts, and the last two at the ends of the two links on the eighth donut.

barcelona

This necklace features a mix of contemporary and natural elements, and it is both ornate and modern. The interesting bail at the center of the pendant is made from a flat piece of filigree with a custom bend.

Designer: Cynthia Deis

Finished size: 18 inches (45.7 cm) long

Materials

1 antiqued brass filigree connector bar with two loops at each end, 10 x 30 mm

2 natural brass filigree bead caps, 12 mm

1 semiprecious labradorite stone oval bead, 16 x 22 mm

1 silver smoke crystal open square bead, 20 mm

15 gray freshwater pearls, 7 mm

1 bright hammered brass round ring, 33 mm

1 bright wavy brass round ring, 15 mm

5 natural brass oval decorative jump rings (from chain), 9 x 5 mm

2 antiqued brass head pins, 1 inch (2.5 cm)

1 antiqued brass spring ring clasp, 1 cm

13½-inch (34.3 cm) length of natural brass rollo chain, 4 x 5 mm

4½-inch (11.4 cm) length of antiqued brass filed tube chain, 13 mm

16-inch (40.6 cm) length of gunmetal 22-gauge craft wire

Tools

Wire cutters

Chain-nose pliers

Round-nose pliers

Instructions

1. Cut the rollo chain into three pieces: one 5¼-inch (13.3 cm), one 4¼-inch (10.8 cm), and one 3½-inch (8.9 cm) length. Set aside.

2. Use chain-nose pliers to grasp the connector bar at its midpoint and make a 45° bend. Slide the connector bar through the open square to check the fit. Determine two even points on the bar to make bends that will accommodate both the crystal and the hammered ring. The end result will be a U shape. Use chain-nose pliers to make the bends (figure 1).

   fig. 1

3. Place the open square, corner side down, into the U shape. Place the hammered ring behind the open square.

4. Pass a head pin through a matching set of the bar's loops, from the open square side (front) to the ring side (back). Form a simple loop to secure the head pin. Repeat for the other set of the bar's loops (figure 2). Set the pendant aside.

   fig. 2

   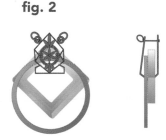

5. Hold a bead cap in one hand as you press the end of the labradorite bead into it, allowing the cap to mold to the stone's shape. Repeat with the other cap.

6. Cut a 4-inch (10.2 cm) piece of wire and form a wrapped loop on one end. Slide on one bead cap from outside to inside the labradorite bead, and another bead cap from inside to outside. Form another wrapped loop to secure the beads. Set the labradorite link aside.

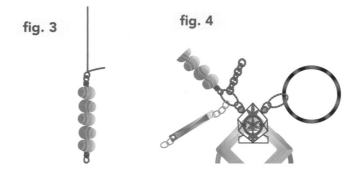

fig. 3

fig. 4

7. Cut a 4-inch (10.2 cm) piece of wire and form a wrapped loop on one end. Slip on five 7-mm beads and form another wrapped loop to secure the beads, creating the first pearl link. Cut another 4-inch (10.2 cm) piece of wire. Make a wrapped loop that attaches to an end loop of the first pearl link (figure 3).

8. Slide on five 7-mm beads and form a wrapped loop to secure the beads. Cut a third 4-inch (10.2 cm) piece of wire and form a wrapped loop that attaches to the open loop at the end of the second pearl link. Slip on the remaining pearl beads and form a wrapped loop. Set the pearl link chain aside.

9. Use a decorative jump ring to connect the pendant's right-side simple loop to the wavy brass ring. Open another decorative jump ring and slip on the pendant's left-side simple loop, one end of the pearl link chain, one end of the tube chain, and one end of the 4¼-inch (10.8 cm) piece of rollo chain. Close the ring (figure 4).

10. Use a decorative jump ring to connect the open ends of the pearl link chain, the tube chain, and the 4¼-inch (10.8 cm) piece of rollo chain to the 3½-inch (8.9 cm) piece of rollo chain. Use chain-nose pliers to open a link at the other end of the 3½-inch (8.9 cm) rollo chain piece and attach it to the clasp. Close the link.

11. Use a decorative jump ring to connect the wavy brass ring to one end of the labradorite link. Use chain-nose pliers to open a link at the end of the 5¼-inch (13.3 cm) piece of rollo chain. Attach the link to the remaining loop on the labradorite link. Attach a decorative jump ring to the other end of the rollo chain.

turtle story

A Native American tradition holds that the world was formed on the back of a turtle. You'll have to make up your own story to explain where the second turtle on this focal bead came from.

Designers: Elizabeth Glass Geltman and Rachel Geltman

Finished size: 27 inches (68.6 cm) long

Materials

35-inch (89.9 cm) length of 16-gauge sterling silver round wire

20-inch (50.8 cm) length of beading wire

8 sterling silver crimp beads

48 sterling silver Bali daisy spacer beads

4 strands hessonite garnets, each 16 inches (40.6 cm) long

2 sterling silver bead cones

Petrified wood beads, ranging from 6 to 10 mm

6 sterling silver Bali bead caps in two different styles

Carved bone turtle bead

S clasp

Tools

Ruler or tape measure

Wire cutters

Chain-nose pliers

Round-nose pliers

Crimping pliers

Cup burr or needle file

Mandrel or small marker (optional)

Steel bench block or anvil (optional)

Rawhide, plastic, or chasing hammer (optional)

Instructions

1. Use the wire cutters to cut two 3-inch (7.6 cm) lengths of 16-gauge sterling silver round wire.

2. With the chain-nose and round-nose pliers, create a wrapped loop at one end of the first wire. Repeat with the second wire. Set the second wire aside.

3. Cut 20 inches (50.8 cm) of beading wire. Feed the beading wire through the loop at the end of one of the pieces of prepared silver round wire, add a crimp bead to the beading wire, and crimp with the crimping pliers.

4. Next, slide two sterling silver Bali daisy spacer beads onto the beading wire. Then string one 16-inch (40.6 cm) strand of hessonite garnets and Bali spacer beads in the desired pattern. Crimp the other end of the beading wire onto the loop of the second piece of round silver wire.

5. Repeat steps 3 and 4 until all four bead strands are strung with hessonite garnets and Bali spacer beads and attached to the loops at the end of both pieces of the round silver wire.

6. Pick up the piece of round silver wire and feed it through the bead cone; wrap the silver wire end to secure. Trim as needed. File the ends with the cup burr or needle file until smooth. The bead cone should hide the four crimped ends.

7. Repeat at the other end of the strung necklace.

8. Cut 3 inches (7.6 cm) of silver round wire. Feed the silver wire through the end loop of your project necklace and create a wrapped loop. Slide a 10-mm petrified wood bead onto the silver round wire, and wrap to secure. This step will begin the process of attaching the wire-wrapped portion to the strung portion of the necklace.

9. Cut 5 inches (12.7 cm) of silver round wire, feed the silver wire through the end loop of your project necklace, and create a wrapped loop. Slide a Bali bead cap, a 10-mm petrified wood bead, and a matching Bali bead cap onto the silver wire. Slide the bone turtle bead onto the open

end of the silver round wire and create a large wire wrap to secure. Trim as necessary and file smooth.

10. Cut another 5 inches (12.7 cm) of the sterling silver round wire, feed the wire through the second hole in the bone turtle bead, and create a large wire wrap to secure. Slide a Bali bead cap, a 10-mm petrified wood bead, and a matching Bali bead cap onto the wire, and wrap to secure.

11. Cut 3 more inches (7.6 cm) of silver round wire. Feed the wire through the end loop of your project necklace, and create a wrapped loop. Slide a 10-mm petrified wood bead onto the wire, and wrap to secure.

12. Repeat step 11, this time sliding a different-style Bali bead cap, a 10-mm petrified wood bead, and a matching Bali bead cap onto the wire, and wrap to secure.

13. At the opposite end of the necklace, repeat step 8.

14. Attach the clasp to the necklace.

Designer's Tips

This necklace is strung to be asymmetrical. You can wear it with the turtle bead centered if you wish, or put the turtle to one side for a different look.

You can create your own S clasps. First, cut 2 inches (5.1 cm) of 16-gauge sterling silver round wire. File both ends of the wire until it's smooth, using a needle file or cup burr. Wrap one end of the wire around the end of a mandrel. (A small marker or thick pencil works well as a mandrel.) Then wrap the other end of the wire around the mandrel in the opposite direction. Harden the wire by hitting it on an anvil with a hammer or mallet. Finally, adjust the clasp with your pliers as necessary until it's the desired size and shape.

twilight

Graceful strands of soft blue and gray gemstones provide the
perfect setting for an eye-catching blistered pearl pendant.

Designer: Valérie MacCarthy

Finished size: 19 inches (48.3 cm) long

Materials

1 blistered pearl pendant, 45 mm

10 light blue chalcedony nuggets, 18 mm

15 gray pearls, 8 mm

6 light blue crystals, 12 mm

7 light blue crystals, 10 mm

1 sterling silver lobster clasp

1 sterling silver ball-end head pin, 1 inch (2.5 cm) long

30-inch (76.2 cm) length of sterling silver chain, 1.5 mm

2½-inch (5.1 cm) length of sterling silver chain (for the toggle), 2.5 mm

55-inch (139.7 cm) length of 24-gauge sterling silver wire

Tools

Chain-nose pliers

Round-nose pliers

Wire cutters

Ruler

Instructions

1. The three strands of this necklace should be approximately 14 inches (35.6 cm), 15½ inches (39.4 cm), and 17 inches (43.2 cm), respectively. While working on each strand, keep a ruler handy for measuring your work as needed.

2. Begin work on the 14-inch (35.6 cm) strand. Make a twisted wire loop, using the round-nose pliers to hold the 24-gauge wire about ¾ inch (1.9 cm) from the end. Place one end of the 30-inch (76.2 cm), 1.5-mm silver chain onto the loop. Hold the loop with the round-nose pliers and twist the wires together. Cut off the shorter wire end. Cut the chain so a length of about 1½ inches (3.8 cm) of chain remains connected to the wire loop.

3. Slide one 8-mm gray pearl onto the wire. Use the round-nose pliers to bend the wire 45°, and then wrap it around. Place one end of the remaining 1.5-mm chain onto this loop. Using the chain-nose pliers, hold the loop and wrap it around to secure. Cut off the excess wire and trim the chain to a length of about 1 inch (2.5 cm).

4. Make a new loop in the wire, place it onto the end of the 1-inch (2.5 cm) piece of chain, and twist the wire around with the chain-nose pliers. Slide on one 10-mm light blue crystal, followed by another 8-mm gray pearl. Again bend the wire 45°, loop it around on the round-nose pliers, and attach it to another chain length about 1½ inches (3.8 cm) long. Once the chain is hanging from the loop, hold the loop with the chain-nose pliers and wrap the wire around to secure. Cut off the excess wire. Make a new wire loop at the end of this chain.

5. Attach an 18-mm chalcedony nugget to the wire. Before continuing to make the strand, pause for a moment to hold this to your neck to make sure you are pleased with how the chain and beads are coming together. Once you've added another length of chain, follow by perhaps adding a 12-mm light blue crystal bead, varying between the 10- and 12-mm crystal beads and gray pearls as you work.

6. Keep working all the way around in this manner until you've completed the 14-inch (35.6 cm) strand. Set it aside.

The design and construction of this necklace is very free once you determine the placement of the ten 18-mm chalcedony nuggets. These need to be placed on the three strands somewhat symmetrically (but not perfectly) so the necklace falls correctly (figure 1).

Then you can place the smaller beads in a random fashion, allowing 1 to 2 inches (2.5 to 5.1 cm) of chain between the various elements. I recommend that you periodically hold the unfinished piece to your neck so you can see how the necklace is progressing. You may want to make changes to the length of the chain segments, adjusting them to be longer or shorter, or to the selection and placement of the stones.

fig. 1

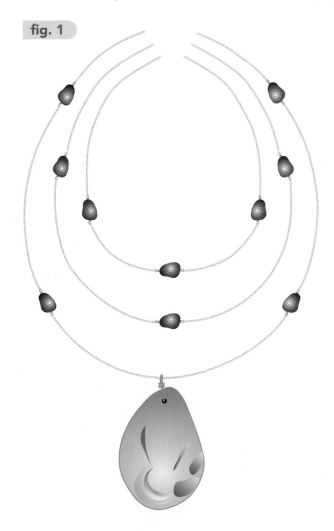

7. Begin the 15½-inch (39.4 cm) strand, working in the same manner of attaching the beads and chain as for the first strand, using steps 2 through 6 as a guide. To see how it falls, hold the chain ends of the first and second strands together. It's important to frequently evaluate how the strands fall together so you can balance the bead placement and chain lengths as you work.

8. For the third strand, the blistered pearl pendant will be attached in the center. If you follow the suggested lengths, the center of the 17-inch (43.2 cm) strand will be 8½ inches (21.6 cm) from the end. To attach the pendant, slide the wire through the bead hole, allowing ¾ inch (1.9 cm) to pass through. Bend both ends up. Bend the two wires again at the top so they cross tightly and twist them around to secure (figure 2). Cut off the shorter wire end.

fig. 2

9. Using the round-nose pliers, make a loop in the wire and slide it to the 8½-inch (21.6 cm) mark on the third strand of the necklace. With the chain-nose pliers, hold the loop and wrap the wire around the twist you made in step 8. Cut off the excess wire.

10. Make the third strand in the same manner of attaching the beads and chain as for the first strand, using steps 2 through 6 as a guide.

11. After you've completed all three strands of the necklace, use the round-nose pliers to make a new loop in the wire. Place all three chain ends onto this loop. Hold the loop with the chain-nose pliers and twist the wires around to secure. Cut off the shorter wire end.

12. Use the round-nose pliers to loop the wire around again. Place the lobster clasp onto this loop. Hold the loop with the chain-nose pliers and wrap the wire around the twist you made in step 11. Cut off the excess wire.

13. Pick up the other end of the necklace and place all three of these chain ends onto a new wire loop made with the round-nose pliers. Repeat the same process as in step 12 of twisting the wires around and making a new loop.

14. Place the 2½ inches (5.1 cm) of 2.5-mm silver chain onto the loop you made in step 13.

15. Hold the wire loop with the chain-nose pliers and wrap the wire around the twist you made in step 13. Cut off the excess wire.

16. Use the 1-inch (2.5 cm) head pin to add a detail on the end of the toggle. Slide a 10-mm light blue crystal bead onto the head pin. Bend the wire of the head pin 45°, hold it with the round-nose pliers, and then loop it around. Attach the loop to the last link in the toggle chain. Holding the loop with the chain-nose pliers, wrap the wire around to secure, and then cut off the excess wire.

kikuyu

Kenya is a common source for batik bones, which are combined here with a variety of intriguing brass beads.

Instructions

1. Straighten the wire with nylon pliers, if necessary.

2. Feed the medium brass bead onto the wire. Create a simple loop at one end of the wire, using your chain-nose and round-nose pliers. Slide the bead so that it's flush against the loop. Create a loop on the other side of the bead (figure 1). Cut the wire with a flush or side wire cutter. Use the chain-nose pliers to adjust the loops so they are tight against the bead. File wire ends smooth where needed.

   fig. 1

3. Repeat step 2, connecting your new loop to the last one you made. This time feed five batik bone beads onto the wire, bending the wire so that the five beads are slightly arced.

4. Repeat the process described in step 2, stringing the beads in the following order:
   - Three batik bone beads
   - Medium brass bead
   - Large batik bone bead
   - Five batik bone beads (Remember to bend the wire so the beads are slightly arced.)
   - Large brass bead
   - Five batik bone beads (Remember to bend the wire so the beads are slightly arced.)
   - Three batik bone beads
   - Small brass bead
   - Large brass bead
   - Three batik bone beads
   - Large brass bead
   - Large batik bone bead
   - Three batik bone beads

5. Attach the pieces of the clasp to both ends of the necklace.

Designers: Elizabeth Glass Geltman and Rachel Geltman

Finished size: 22 inches (55.9 cm) long

Materials

16-gauge brass round wire

2 small brass beads

32 assorted batik bone beads

1 medium brass bead

2 large batik bone beads

3 large brass beads

Clasp

Tools

Nylon pliers

Chain-nose pliers

Round-nose pliers

Flush or side wire cutters

Needle file or cup burr

Mandrel or small marker (optional)

Steel bench block or anvil (optional)

Rawhide, plastic, or chasing hammer (optional)

Designer's Tip

Metals are expensive. To avoid loss when creating jewelry, don't cut a length of wire and then trim the excess. Instead, work directly from the wire spool and then cut the wire to the exact fit.

vortex

Like small whirlpools, silver links swirl around the beads in this necklace. The designer married a large turquoise pendant to a chain crafted entirely of handmade links.

Designer: Mami Laher

Finished size: 17 inches (43.2 cm)

Materials

1 flat turquoise bead,
1¼ inches (3.2 cm)

6 round turquoise beads, 1 cm

2 faceted turquoise beads, 7 mm

10-foot (3.1 m) length of 18-gauge
sterling silver wire

58 sterling silver jump rings,
18-gauge, 5 mm

Tools

Wire cutters

Tape measure

Flat-nose pliers

2 pairs of round-nose pliers

Hammer and block

Instructions

1. Cut a piece of wire 6 inches (15.2 cm)
    long. On one end, make a spiral. Thread
    the large bead on the wire, then bend
    just the spiral around the end of the
    stone to cup the front of it. On the
    other end of the bead, make a wrapped
    loop. Cut the wire tail 1½ inches
    (3.8 cm) long and form it into a spiral.
    Bend this spiral to cup the top of the bead.

2. Cut four pieces of wire, each 3 inches
    (7.6 cm) long. Make four bead links
    shaped like figure 1, two with round
    beads on them and two with faceted
    beads on them. After you've finished
    the initial wire shaping, forge each link's
    curve at its apex, as shown by the wider
    areas in the illustration (if the link loses
    its form during this process, simply
    readjust its shape with pliers). These are
    A links.

fig. 1

3. Cut four pieces of wire, each 4½ inches (11.4 cm) long. Using a round bead on each, fashion bead links shaped like figure 2, forging the apexes of the curves, as shown. These are B links.

4. Cut 20 pieces of wire, each 3½ inches (8.9 cm) long. Shape each into a link as you did in step 3, but without a bead on it. These are C links.

5. To make the clasp, cut a piece of wire 2¼ inches (5.7 cm) long. Shape and forge it as shown in figure 3, then forge the outer curves.

6. Make half of the chain by joining the links with pairs of jump rings, keeping each one oriented as shown in the photograph. Use two jump rings to attach each link to the next, with the jump ring at the top connecting through the center of the spiraled area of one link and the curved part of the next, and the jump ring at the bottom likewise connecting the links in a mirrored fashion. Join them in the following order: A C B C B C C C C C C C

C A. The first A link should be one with a round bead on it, and the last A link should have a faceted one. Repeat to make the other half of the chain.

7. Place one chain on the work surface, with the links laid out in the sequence from the previous step. To its left, place the other chain so it mirrors the first. Keeping the chain pieces in this orientation, attach both of the round-bead A links to the wrapped loop of the centerpiece, using jump rings through their spirals. Then use a jump ring to attach the forged curves of both A links together.

8. On one end of the chain, use a jump ring to attach the clasp. Attach the two remaining jump rings, one linked to the other, to the other end of the chain.

fig. 2

fig. 3

helen

If Marie Antoinette were around, she'd beg you for this glamorous necklace. The mix of colors and beads makes it the perfect accompaniment for a simple formal dress as well as a fun piece to wear with more casual clothes.

Designer: Cynthia Deis

Finished size: 28 inches (71.1 cm) long

Materials

1 antiqued brass dapped filigree square cross, 50 mm

1 antiqued brass filigree ring, 32 mm

2 antiqued brass dapped filigree rosettes, 28 mm

2 antiqued brass dapped filigree six-point flowers, 22 mm

2 antiqued brass flat filigree six-point flowers, 22 mm

1 antiqued brass dapped filigree eight-point oval, 36 x 48 mm

1 antiqued brass dapped five-point filigree flower, 20 mm

1 antiqued brass flat five-point filigree flower, 20 mm

1 blue dyed semiprecious jade oval cabochon, 18 x 36 mm

1 white opal crystal round bead, 8 mm

6 light pink crystal bicone beads, 6 mm

6 light blue opal crystal bicone beads, 6 mm

1 light red crystal round bead, 6 mm

11 aqua fire-polished glass round beads, 6 mm

9 acid-green glass druk beads, 6 mm

31 fuchsia crystal round beads, 4 mm

8 acid-green fire-polished glass round beads, 4 mm

(Continued on next page)

Instructions

1. Slide one green druk bead onto a head pin. Add one bead cap, inside to outside, and form a simple loop to secure the bead and cap. Repeat to create seven green bead dangles. Set aside.

   Repeat to create six aqua fire-polished bead dangles.

2. Cut a 1½-inch (3.8 cm) length of craft wire. Form a simple loop at one end. Slip on one bead cap from outside to inside, one green druk bead, and one bead cap from inside to outside. Form a simple loop to secure the caps and bead. Set the green bead link aside.

   Repeat once to make another green bead link. Repeat twice using 6-mm aqua beads.

3. Open a loop on a green bead link and attach it to one end of the chain. Close the loop. Attach the other end of the same bead link to an aqua bead link. Repeat for the other end of the chain. Set aside.

4. Cut a 12-inch (38.5 cm) length of beading wire. Place the rosettes back to back, edges aligned. Pass the beading wire through a hole at the edge of the two pieces and tie a square knot, leaving a 4-inch (10.2 cm) tail, as shown in figure 1.

   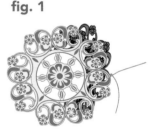

   fig. 1

   String one 4-mm fuchsia bead onto the long end of the wire and sew around the edge of the paired rosettes, passing through the next hole as you go (figure 2). Make sure the beads stay on the side of the rosette and don't move to the front or back. Repeat around to add sixteen 4-mm beads in all. Tie a square knot with the working and tail wires and trim close to the knot.

   fig. 2

   Attach the square jump ring to one side of the rosette and an oval jump ring to the opposite side. Set the beaded rosette aside.

Materials (continued)

16 turquoise blue fire-polished glass round beads, 4 mm

45 light red crystal round beads, 3 mm

21 antiqued brass petal bead caps, 4 x 6 mm

15 antiqued brass head pins, 1 inch (2.5 cm)

12 antiqued brass round jump rings, 5 mm

19 antiqued brass extra thick oval jump rings, 5 x 6 mm

1 antiqued brass square jump ring, 12 mm

12-inch (38.5 cm) length of antiqued brass chain, 5 x 6 mm

6½-yard (5.9 m) length of medium-width flexible beading wire

6-inch (15.2 cm) length of gunmetal 20-gauge craft wire

Paper and pencil

Tools

Chain-nose pliers

Round-nose pliers

Wire cutters

5. Cut a 12-inch (30.5 cm) length of wire and string on a light red 6-mm round bead, leaving a 4-inch (10.2 cm) tail. Sew the bead to the center of a dapped six-point flower. Tie a square knot on the back of the flower to firmly seat the bead (figure 3).

fig. 3

Pass the long wire end to the front of the flower, exiting from a petal. String on one 6-mm blue opal bicone bead and sew it to the petal (figure 4). Repeat around to add six blue opal beads in all. Tie a square knot on the back of the flower and trim the excess wire.

fig. 4

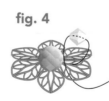

Place the beaded flower on top of a flat six-point flower, backs touching and edges aligned. Use round jump rings to attach the flat and dapped petals at each of the six points (figure 5). Set aside.

fig. 5

Repeat this step to make another six-point beaded flower, this time using a 6-mm aqua bead for the center and 6-mm pink bicone beads for the petals.

6. Cut an 8-inch (20.3 cm) length of beading wire. String on the 8-mm white opal bead and slide it to the center of the wire. Pass the wire ends through the dapped oval so the bead is seated in the center. Pass the wire ends up through the filigree, knot securely, and trim the ends very close. *Note:* The knot is placed on the oval's front because the oval's back will be exposed in the finished design.

fig. 6

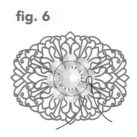

Cut a 12-inch (30.5 cm) length of beading wire and string on eight 4-mm green beads, leaving a 4-inch (10.2 cm) tail. Tie a square knot to make a tight circle of beads. Place the circle around the white opal bead and pass the wire ends down through the filigree. Pass the long wire end up through the filigree between the next two beads in the circle. Cross over the wire between beads and pass back down through the filigree (figure 6). Continue in this manner to completely sew the circle to the oval. Use the working and tail wires to tie a tight square knot and trim.

fig. 7

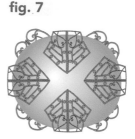

Attach one oval jump ring to one end of the filigree oval and two evenly spaced oval jump rings to the opposite side. Set the filigree oval aside.

7. Lay the cross face down on the work surface. Place the cabochon, face up, in the center of the cross. Decide where you'd like the points of the cross to bend up and over the cabochon. It may be useful to sketch the shape of the filigree and note the bend points on the sketch while working. Remove the cabochon. Use chain-nose pliers to gently bend the points of the filigree up to form right angles. Place the cabochon back into the center of the cross. Working from side to side, use chain-nose pliers to slowly and carefully bend each point over the cabochon (figure 7). Take care to not scratch the stone's surface with the pliers. *Note:* If the cabochon is loose, use chain-nose pliers to carefully tighten the fit, continuing to work side to side, not clockwise. To create an even setting, make many small adjustments rather than a few large ones.

fig. 8

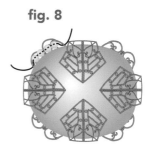

Cut a 4-inch (10.2 cm) length of beading wire and string on four 4-mm aqua beads. Slide them to the center. Working from the front of the filigree on one corner of the cabochon, pass both ends of the wire through the filigree holes (figure 8). Tie a square knot to secure the beads. Trim the excess wire. Repeat to add four beads to each corner.

Attach two evenly spaced oval jump rings to one end of the cross and a matching set on the opposite side. Set the jade oval aside.

fig. 9

8. Cut a 6-inch (15.2 cm) length of beading wire and string on five 4-mm fuchsia beads, leaving a 2-inch (5.1 cm) tail. Tie a square knot to make a tight bead circle. Center the circle on the dapped five-point flower and pass the wire ends down through the filigree. Pass the long wire up through the filigree and sew the circle down using the technique in figure 6. Knot the wire ends and trim.

Cut a 12-inch (30.5 cm) length of beading wire and pass it up through the filigree, exiting from the base of one of the petals and leaving a 4-inch (10.2 cm) tail. String on two 3-mm light red beads and pass down through the filigree so the beads sit side by side. Tie a square knot to secure the beads. This is row 1. Lay the wire across the back of the petal and pass up through the filigree, exiting just down the petal from the first bead strung. Repeat to make row 2, using one 3-mm light red bead, one 4-mm fuchsia bead, and one 3-mm light red bead (figure 9). Continue making rows in this order: row 3, two 3-mm light red beads; row 4, three 3-mm light red beads; and row 5, one 4-mm fuchsia bead. Tie a square knot with the wire ends and trim. Repeat for the remaining petals.

Stack the beaded flower and a flat five-point flower, backs touching. Cut a 12-inch (30.5 cm) length of wire. Use a square knot to attach the wire near the base of a petal on the flat flower, leaving a 4-inch (10.2 cm) tail. Use the long wire to sew the edges of the top and bottom flowers together. Maintain a tight tension. When you reach the starting point, tie the wire ends in a square knot (figure 10). Trim the wire ends.

Attach two oval jump rings to the end of one petal. Count two petals over and add one jump ring. Set the beaded five-point flower aside.

9. Pass a head pin through the edge of a filigree ring from inside to outside (figure 11).

   Slip on one 6-mm aqua bead and form a wrapped loop to secure the bead. Repeat for the opposite side of the ring (figure 12). Set the beaded ring aside.

10. Lay out the necklace elements in the order they were created, from steps 4 through 9. Make sure the pieces are all face up. Use one oval jump ring to connect each of the elements to the oval jump rings already placed on the pieces. *Note:* You'll need to connect the beaded ring by attaching oval jump rings to the wrapped loops.

11. Connect a bead link at the end of the chain to the square jump ring on the rosette. Attach the bead link at the other end of the chain to the round jump ring opposite the oval jump ring placed on the blue six-point flower.

12. Attach the bead dangles to the necklace in this order: two green dangles to the bottom two points of the pink six-point flower; three aqua dangles to the bottom of the filigree oval, making sure they're evenly spaced; one aqua and one green dangle to the bottom left of the cabochon oval, and one green and one aqua dangle to the bottom right; two green dangles to the petal nearest the cabochon oval; and one aqua and one green dangle to the bottom two points of the blue six-point flower.

fig. 10

fig. 11

fig. 12

city nights

Step out in style when you wear this exceptional necklace, a showpiece design made with jasper and garnets.

Designer: Valérie MacCarthy

Finished size: Each strand, from shortest to longest: 18½ inches (47 cm); 23 inches (58.4 cm); 30 inches (76.2 cm)

Materials

10 ocean jasper beads, 14 mm

10 ocean jasper beads, 10 mm

5 ocean jasper beads, 8 mm

8 ocean jasper beads, 6 mm

10 honey jasper beads, 8 mm

18 garnet beads, 6 mm

10 rutile quartz beads, 4 mm

12 carnelian beads, 4 mm

1 gold-filled lobster clasp

75-inch (190.5 cm) length of 1.5-mm gold-filled chain

4-inch (10.2 cm) length of 22-gauge gold-filled wire

130-inch (330.2 cm) length of 24-gauge gold-filled wire

Tools

Chain-nose pliers

Round-nose pliers

Wire cutters

Large rubberized round-nose pliers

Ruler

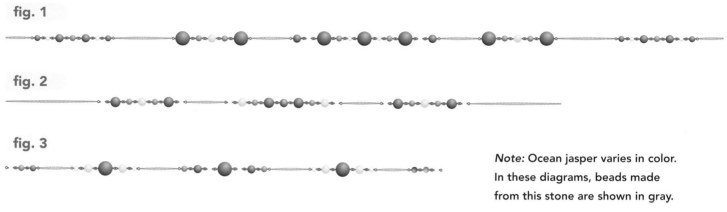

fig. 1

fig. 2

fig. 3

Note: Ocean jasper varies in color. In these diagrams, beads made from this stone are shown in gray.

Instructions

1. Begin this necklace by making the longest strand, following the diagram in figure 1. Cut the chain to make 18 segments in the following lengths: six short segments each 1 inch (2.5 cm), six medium segments each 1½ inches (3.8 cm), and six long segments each 2¼ inches (5.7 cm). Count the links to make sure each segment is exactly the same length. You'll be adding the segments in groups of three. After the segments are attached at one end and you are ready to attach them at the other end, I recommend that you hang the strand so the chains will be dangling as you slide on the connecting wire loop. This helps ensure that the chain segments will be perfectly straight and not twisted or tangled as you attach them.

2. Make a loop in the 24-gauge wire about ¾ inch (1.9 cm) from the end using the round-nose pliers. Slide the end links of three 1-inch (2.5 cm) chain segments onto the wire loop. Hold the loop with the chain-nose pliers and twist the wire around to secure. Cut off the shorter wire end.

3. Slide on one 6-mm ocean jasper bead. Bend the wire 45° and loop it around using the round-nose pliers. Hold the loop with the chain-nose pliers and wrap the wire around to secure. Cut off the excess wire. Repeat the process of adding individual twisted wire bead links to the strand by making a new loop with the wire, sliding it into the loop you just completed, and placing the next bead. Follow this order: 4-mm rutile quartz bead, 8-mm jasper bead, 6-mm garnet bead, 8-mm jasper bead, 4-mm rutile quartz bead, 6-mm jasper bead. Before you close the loop for the last 6-mm jasper bead, slide on three 2¼-inch (5.7 cm) chain segments.

4. Make a new loop in the wire and slide the end links of the chain segments onto it. Add the next group of individual twisted wire bead links in this order: 14-mm jasper bead, 6-mm garnet bead, 8-mm honey jasper bead, 6-mm garnet bead, and 14-mm jasper bead. Before you close the loop for the last 14-mm jasper bead, slide on three 1½-inch (3.8 cm) chain segments.

5. Make a new loop in the wire and slide the end links of the chain segments onto it. Add the next group of individual twisted wire bead links in this order: 8-mm jasper bead, 4-mm carnelian bead, 14-mm jasper bead, 6-mm garnet bead, 4-mm rutile quartz bead, 14-mm jasper bead, 4-mm rutile quartz bead, 6-mm garnet bead, 14-mm jasper bead, 4-mm carnelian bead, and 8-mm jasper bead. Before you close the loop for the last 8-mm jasper bead, slide on three 1½-inch (3.8 cm) chain segments. The 14-mm jasper bead in the middle of this segment is the center of this strand.

6. To complete this strand, you'll add the same group of individual twisted wire bead links that you added in step 4, but this time you'll slide on three

2¼-inch (5.7 cm) chain segments. Then, you'll finish by adding the same group of individual twisted wire bead links that you added in step 3, sliding on the remaining three 1-inch (2.5 cm) chain segments. You should now have a perfectly symmetrical strand.

7. Now that you've finished the long strand, set it aside and make the medium and short ones. After all three are finished, you will attach them together.

8. For the medium strand, follow figure 2. Cut the chain to make 12 segments in the following lengths: six short segments each 1½ inches (3.8 cm) and six long segments each 3½ inches (8.9 cm). Follow the directions in step 1 for counting the links and attaching the chain segments.

9. Make a loop in the 24-gauge wire about ¾ inch (1.9 cm) from the end using the round-nose pliers. Slide the end links of three 3½-inch (8.9 cm) chain segments onto the wire loop. Hold the loop with the chain-nose pliers and twist the wire around to secure. Cut off the shorter wire end.

10. Slide on one 4-mm carnelian bead. Bend the wire 45° and loop it around using the round-nose pliers. Hold the loop with the chain-nose pliers and wrap the wire around to secure. Cut off the excess wire. Repeat the process of adding individual twisted wire bead links to the strand by making a new loop with the wire, sliding it into the loop you just completed, and placing the next bead. Follow this order: 10-mm ocean jasper bead, 6-mm garnet bead, 8-mm honey jasper bead, 6-mm garnet bead, 10-mm ocean jasper bead, and 4-mm carnelian bead. Before you close the loop for the last 4-mm carnelian bead, slide on three 1½-inch (3.8 cm) chain segments.

11. Make a new loop in the wire and slide the end links of the chain segments onto it. Add the next group of individual twisted wire bead links in this order: 4-mm carnelian bead, 8-mm honey jasper bead, 6-mm garnet

bead, 10-mm ocean jasper bead, 8-mm ocean jasper bead, 10-mm ocean jasper bead, 6-mm garnet bead, 8-mm honey jasper bead, and 4-mm carnelian bead. Before you close the loop for the last 4-mm carnelian bead, slide on the three remaining 1½-inch (3.8 cm) chain segments. The 8-mm ocean jasper bead in the middle of this segment is the center of this strand.

12. To complete this strand, you'll add the same group of individual twisted wire bead links that you added in step 9, but this time you'll slide on the remaining three 3½-inch (8.9 cm) chain segments.

13. Now that you've finished the medium strand, set it aside and make the short one.

14. To make the short strand, see figure 3. Cut the chain to make six segments in the following lengths: six segments each 1¼ inches (3.2 cm) and six segments each 1½ inches (3.8 cm). Follow the directions in step 1 for counting the links and attaching the chain segments.

15. Make a loop in the 24-gauge wire and place three of the 1¼ inches (3.2 cm) pieces of chain on the loop. Hold the loop with the chain-nose pliers and twist the wires together. Cut off the shorter wire end.

16. Slide one 6-mm jasper bead onto the wire. Bend the wire 45° and loop it around using the round-nose pliers. Hold the loop with the chain-nose pliers and wrap the loop around to secure. Cut off the excess wire.

17. Repeat the process of adding individual twisted wire bead links to the strand by making a new loop with the wire, sliding it into the loop you just completed, and placing the next bead. Add one 6-mm garnet bead and then one 4-mm carnelian bead in this fashion. After you add the carnelian bead, hold the wire loop and wrap it around to secure. Cut off the excess wire.

18. Add twisted wire bead links to the opposite end of the group of chains. Follow this bead order: 4-mm rutile quartz bead, 8-mm honey jasper bead, 14-mm jasper

bead, 8-mm honey jasper bead, and 4-mm rutile quartz bead. Before you close the loop for the last 4-mm quartz bead, slide on three 1½-inch (3.8 cm) chain segments.

19. Repeat the process of adding individual twisted wire bead links to the strand by making a new loop with the wire, sliding it into the end links of the chain segments, and placing the next bead. Add the next group of individual beads in this order: 6-mm garnet bead, 8-mm jasper bead, 4-mm carnelian bead, 14-mm jasper bead, 4-mm carnelian bead, 8-mm jasper bead, and a 6-mm garnet bead. Before you close the loop for the last 6-mm garnet bead, slide on the three remaining 1½-inch (3.8 cm) chain segments. The 14-mm ocean jasper bead in the middle of this segment is the center of this strand.

20. To complete this strand, you'll add the same group of individual twisted wire bead links that you added in step 16, but you'll slide on the remaining three 1¼-inch (3.2 cm) chain segments. Then, you'll finish by adding the same group of individual twisted wire bead links that you added in steps 14 and 15. After adding the final 4-mm carnelian bead, wrap the loop to secure and cut away the excess wire.

21. Make a loop in the 22-gauge wire about ¾ inch (1.9 cm) from the end using the round-nose pliers. Slide this loop through the lobster clasp. Hold the loop with the chain-nose pliers and twist the wires around to secure. Cut off the shorter wire. Slide one 6-mm jasper bead onto the wire and bend the wire 45°. Loop the wire around using the round-nose pliers.

22. Slide all three strands onto this loop in the following order: first, the three chains of the long strand; second, the three chains of the medium strand; and third, the loop at the end of the short strand. Hold the loop containing all your strands with the chain-nose pliers and wrap the wire around to secure. Continue wrapping the wire around several times to add extra looping detail (figure 4). After wrapping the wire around about five times, cut off the excess.

fig. 4

23. Using the 22-gauge wire and the rubberized round-nose pliers, make a large loop about ¾ inch (1.9 cm) from the end. Hold this large loop with these pliers and twist the wires around. Cut off the shorter wire end. String on one 6-mm jasper bead and bend the wire 45°. Loop the wire around using the round-nose pliers.

24. This time, slide the other end of all three strands onto this loop, again using the same order: first, the three chains of the long strand; second, the three chains of the medium necklace; and third, the loop at the end of the short strand. Hold this new loop with the chain-nose pliers and wrap the wire around. Continue wrapping the wire around several times to add extra looping detail. After wrapping the wire around about five times, cut off the excess.

take five

Large faceted gemstones love to take center stage. For this bold
necklace, a double chain is the key ingredient for perfect balance.

Designer: Lisa Colby

Finished size: 22½ inches (57 cm) long

Materials

5 large faceted turquoise beads

30-inch (76 cm) length of sterling silver rolo chain, 3.9 mm

11 sterling silver 16-gauge jump rings, 4 mm

12-inch (30.5 cm) length of 20-gauge sterling silver wire

Toggle clasp

Tools

Round-nose pliers

Needle-nose pliers

Wire cutters

Liver of sulphur

0000 steel wool

Instructions

1. Oxidize the silver chain, toggle clasp, and jump rings for an antiqued look. Dissolve the liver of sulphur in hot water. Add the silver pieces, remove them, and dry thoroughly. Use the steel wool to rub off the dark finish and polish the silver.

2. Using wire cutters, cut the rolo chain into eight 2-inch (5 cm) lengths and four 3½-inch (8.9 cm) lengths.

3. Cut the sterling silver wire into five 2-inch (5.1 cm) lengths. Thread each bead onto a length of wire. Using the round-nose pliers, wrap the end of the wire twice to make double loops on both ends of the bead.

4. Attach a jump ring to each loop. Then attach two 2-inch (5.1 cm) lengths of chain to one end of each bead. Connect the five beads by attaching the double chains to the jump rings on the beads.

5. Attach two 3½-inch (8.9 cm) lengths of rolo chain to each of the remaining jump rings on the end of the string of beads. Using jump rings, attach the ends of the chains to the toggle clasp.

honey drizzle

This three-strand necklace is a great project to highlight a collection of orphan beads and chains from your stash. The clasp is embellished, which gives you the option to wear the toggle up front.

Designer: Janet A. Lasher

Finished size: 20 inches (50.8 cm) long

Materials

5 white potato freshwater pearls, 10 mm

16 golden half-round potato freshwater pearls, 8 mm

8 semiprecious citrine nuggets, 12 mm

16 semiprecious faceted African opal rounds, 5 mm

15 topaz and light topaz crystals in assorted shapes, 3 to 12 mm

6 gold-filled or sterling silver jump rings, 5 mm

1 gold-filled or sterling silver head pin, 3 inches (7.6 cm)

1 gold-filled or sterling silver toggle clasp, 25 mm

Assorted gold-filled or sterling silver chain remnants, 45 inches (1.1 m) total

5-foot (1.5 m) length of 24-gauge gold-filled or sterling silver wire

Silver black or other patina

Paper towel

Tools

Wire cutters

Glass or plastic container for patina

Polishing pads or extra-fine steel wool

Wire-straightening pliers

Measuring tape

Three-strand jewelry design board

Chain-nose pliers

Round-nose pliers

Instructions

1. Cut the 24-gauge wire into pieces, each approximately 12 inches (30.8 cm) long. Set aside.

2. Prepare the patina according to the manufacturer's instructions. Dip the jump rings, head pin, clasp, chain, and wire into the patina. Once you reach the desired effect, remove the pieces and rinse with clear water. Let air dry on a paper towel. *Note:* Don't immerse the beads into the patina; it may permanently remove the nacre on the pearls and mar the surfaces of stones and other beads. Polish each piece of wire, chain, clasp, and head pin with a polishing pad or extra-fine steel wool to achieve an antique look.

3. Run each wire piece through the wire-straightening pliers. This straightens and tempers the wire at the same time. Cut the wire into 3- to 4-inch (7.6 to 10.2 cm) pieces and set aside.

fig. 1

4. Slide a 5-mm crystal and an 8-mm pearl on the head pin. Form a simple loop to secure the beads. Pick up one of the wire pieces and make a wrapped loop at one end that attaches to the simple loop you just created. String on one citrine nugget and form a wrapped loop to secure it (figure 1). Set the dangle aside.

5. Cut the chain remnants into pieces, each 1 to 2 inches (2.5 to 5.1 cm) long.

6. Utilize the bead design board to make a random arrangement of chains and beads or sets of beads, being sure to begin and end the sequence with a chain. Keep in mind that this is a three-strand necklace—each strand can be the same length or you can create a layered look by linking the upper and lower strands off of the middle length of chain. Design all three strands at the same time to achieve a good distribution of chains and beads across the length of the necklace.

7. Use a jump ring to attach one half of the clasp to the end link of the first chain. Form a wrapped loop on the end of one of the wire pieces that attaches to the end link at the other end of this chain. String on the first bead or set of beads in your arrangement and form a wrapped loop that attaches to the end link of the next chain (figure 2). Repeat across to complete the middle strand. Use one jump ring to attach the other half of the clasp to the end link of the last chain.

8. Repeat step 7 to create the second and third strands (figure 3).

9. Attach the dangle to the jump ring at the ring end of the necklace.

10. Check all the wrapped loops for clean cuts and tucked-in wire ends. If desired, use the polishing pad to polish the chains and toggle.

fig. 2

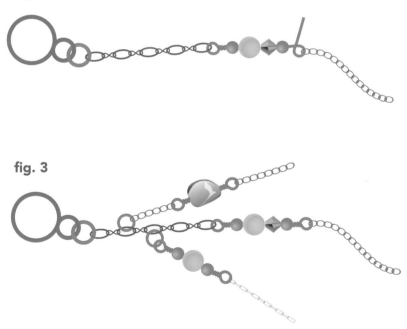

fig. 3

silk road

Use pliers and a jewelry-making jig to plot the twists and turns of the brass wires that link this collection of Chinese porcelain beads.

Designers: Elizabeth Glass Geltman and Rachel Geltman

Finished size: 28 inches (71.1 cm) long

Materials

15-foot (4.6 m) length of 16-gauge brass round wire

19 Chinese porcelain beads in varied sizes, shapes, and colors

Block of wood (optional)

Five nails (optional)

Three tubular beads or objects (optional; cut pipe works well here)

Tools

Chain-nose pliers

Jewelry-making jig

Wire cutters

Cup burr or needle file

Rawhide, plastic, or chasing hammer

Steel bench block or anvil

Ruler or tape measure

Round-nose pliers

Permanent marker (optional)

Instructions

1. This project requires that you make two different patterns out of the brass wire, so you'll need to set up a jig. You can either make your own (see tip box), or use a purchased jewelry-making jig.

2. Use the chain-nose pliers to create a loop at one end of your wire. Place the loop on the jig peg, and then wrap the wire around the jig pegs to create the link. (Figure 1 shows a half-completed link.) Remove the link from the jig, use the wire cutters to trim the wire, and file smooth with cup burr or needle file. Straighten wires as necessary. Harden links with the hammer and anvil or steel block. Repeat until you've created five links in this same shape.

fig. 1

3. Set up the jig for the second link shape and repeat the same process as in step 2 until you've made four links in this second shape.

Designer's Tips

Although it's easy to make your own jig, you can also purchase a jewelry-making jig. The advantage of a manufactured jig is that it's reusable. It also has a clear base, so it's easy to draw a design on a piece of paper and then place the jig over the design to determine where to insert the pegs.

But if you want to make a homemade jig, here's how. Assemble a block of wood, five nails, and three tubular beads or objects (cut pipe works well). Hammer the nails into the block. Slide the beads onto the nails.

4. Set the links aside, and assemble the beaded links. Cut about 2 to 3 inches (5.1 to 7.6 cm) of wire, depending on bead size. Slide the bead onto the wire. Use the round-nose pliers to make a loop on either side of the bead. Trim the wire, and file until smooth to the touch. Adjust the loops with pliers so they are snug against the bead and the loops are nicely rounded. Repeat until you have created 19 beaded links.

5. Assemble the necklace. Using your chain-nose pliers to open the loops, connect your links and beaded loops together to create a chain.

6. To make the clasp, cut 3 inches (7.6 cm) of wire and use the round-nose pliers to make a small loop at one end. Pull the looped end of the wire around your forefinger. Next, while holding the looped end, pull the wire around the forefinger of your other hand. Trim the wire and file until smooth. Pull one end into a scroll shape. Harden with the hammer and anvil or steel block.

7. Attach the clasp.

Designer's Tip

To create uniform-sized loops, mark your pliers with a permanent marker and create the loops on this line.

anemone

Designer Elizabeth Larsen evokes an exotic sea creature with this high-contrast necklace. Her elegant method of wrapping snow jade beads with tendrils of black, spiraled wire makes a stunning piece.

Designer: Elizabeth Larsen

Finished size: 17 inches (43.2 cm) long

Materials

148 round white jade beads, 6 mm

84 round white jade beads, 8 mm

36 round white jade beads, 10 mm

12-foot (3.7 m) length of 20-gauge round sterling silver wire, for the jump rings

134-foot (40.8 m) length of 24-gauge round black wire, for the wrapped bead loops

1 fancy "wave"-style clasp

Hypo cement adhesive for nonporous surfaces

Glue, dab

Tools

Knitting needle, 2.75 mm (size 2 U.S.)

Wire cutters

2 pairs of needle-nose pliers

Tape measure

Round-nose pliers

Flat-nose pliers (optional)

Instructions

1. Using the 20-gauge silver wire and the knitting needle, make 274 jump rings. Link the jump rings two by two to make a chain 15 inches (38.1 cm) long. Attach each half of the clasp to either end with jump rings. Set the chain aside.

2. Cut a piece of black wire 6 inches (15.2 cm) long. Using round-nose pliers, form a loop at one end. Add a white jade bead to the wire, then form a second loop. Hold this second loop with a pair of flat-nose or needle-nose pliers and loosely spiral the remaining wire around the bead with your free hand. Fasten the wire around the base of the first loop with one full wrap, then cut off any extra wire. Use needle-nose pliers to secure the end of the wire snugly around the base of the loop and secure it with a dab of glue. Figure 1 shows the finished element. Repeat for each bead. Depending on the bead's diameter, you may need more or less than 6 inches (15.2 cm) of wire for each.

3. To attach the beads to the chain, start at one end of the chain. Open a jump ring in the first pair, slip on two 6-mm wire-wrapped beads by their loops, and close the jump ring. Open the other jump ring from the same pair, attach it to the same loops of the wrapped beads, and close it. Repeat for all the pairs of jump rings, first attaching half the 6-mm beads, then half the 8-mm beads. Attach all the 10-mm beads, then the remainder of the 8-mm ones, and finally, the rest of the 6-mm beads.

fig. 1

dancing branches

Capture the appearance of buds on bare branches in spring with this delicate necklace that nestles on your collarbone.

Designer: Kathy Frey

Finished size: 16 to 18 inches
(40.6 to 45.7 cm) long

Materials

3-foot (91.4 cm) length of 24- or
22-gauge half-hard sterling silver
wire (use the heaviest gauge that
fits your beads)

Clasp

25–30 semiprecious stone, glass, or
pearl beads in a variety of shapes,
colors, sizes, and finishes

Tools

Wire cutters

Chain-nose pliers

Flat-nose pliers

Designer's Tip

A free-form necklace like this
is easier achieved by thinking
about the individual components. When making links, mix
up the lengths. Make short
links—each ½ to ¾ inch (1.2 to
1.9 cm)—to help smooth out
the curve between some larger
1½-inch (3.8 cm) links, and
add some sizes in between.
(The link lengths are all ap-
proximate.) Working this way
is a good trick for fighting our
natural tendency to make
symmetrical patterns!

Instructions

1. When making the branch links,
make the small, simple links
first. Use wire cutters to flush trim
the tip of the 3-foot (91.4 cm)
wire and form a simple loop at
the trimmed end. Thread a bead,
and leaving some empty space
on the wire, use wire cutters to
flush cut the other end to loop
length. Make a simple loop at
this end perpendicular to the
first loop.

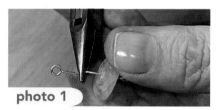

photo 1

2. Use chain-nose pliers to bend
one or two kinks in the wire to
position the bead where you
want it—moved to one end or
suspended in the middle. Bend
only enough to prevent the
bead from sliding over the kink
(photo 1).

3. Repeat steps 1 and 2 to create
six to eight simple links. Make
each one slightly different from
the others by varying the link
length, bead type, and/or bead
position. When planning your
necklace, keep in mind that
you'll need a couple of small
bead links near the clasp and a
few short links near the bends
in the necklace, where it drapes
around the neck.

4. Create larger links. These can each have only
one large bead on its own or several beads,
with kinks separating or grouping them.
Have fun making a variety of simple combi-
nations on each branch, such as one link
with a small-large combination, one with a
dark-light-dark combination, and another
with a translucent-opaque combination.
Focus on the individual branches at this
point and making each one different to
achieve a more random look.

5. When your branches are finished, connect
them to one another. Use flat-nose pliers to
open the simple loop at one end of the link
(as you would a jump ring); attach the next
link by passing one of its end loops over
the first link's open loop; close the loop;
and repeat. Start and end with the small
bead links that will connect to the clasp.
Again, try not to create a pattern—just link
together what comes to hand.

6. When the branches reach your desired
necklace length, hold the length in place
around your neck, and check to see if you
are pleased with the design and how it
drapes. Reposition the branches as needed.
For instance, if a heavy bead falls too close
to the center and pulls the necklace in an
awkward direction, move that branch farther
away from the center. Or if a dark bead
lands right in the center of the necklace,
creating too much of a focal point, you may
want to move the branch elsewhere.

7. Attach the clasp.

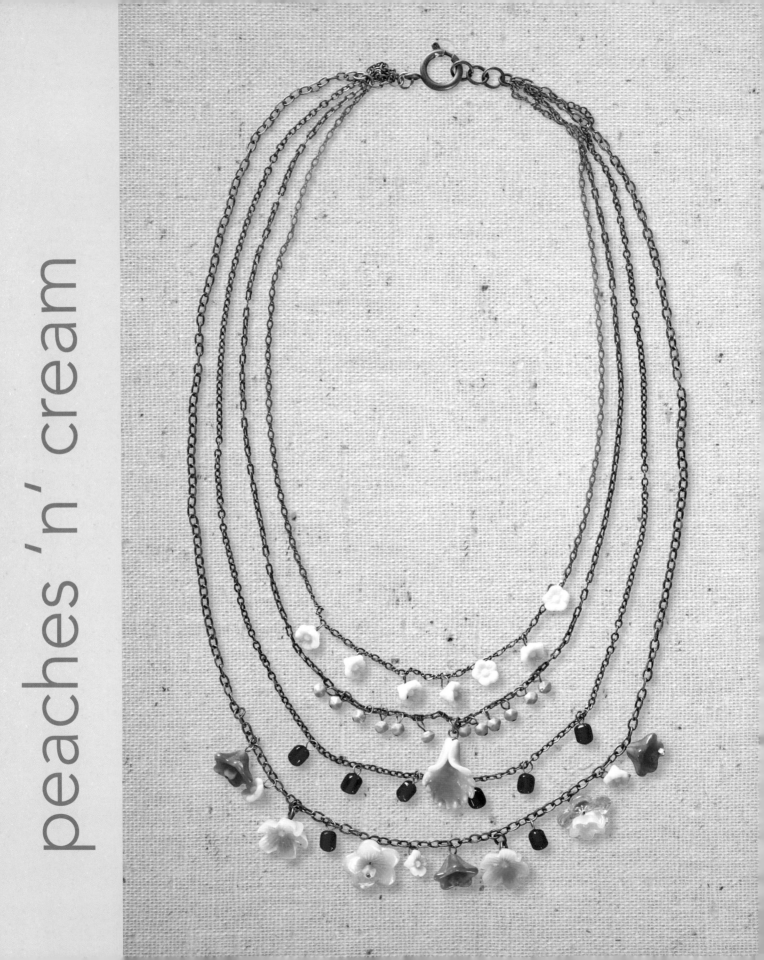

peaches 'n' cream

You'll collect a large number of flower and leaf beads for this necklace. Either stick with a limited color palette as shown, or mix it up to make your necklace full of different flavors.

Designer: Kaari Meng

Finished size: 22 inches (55.9 cm) long

Materials

10 eggshell flower-shaped glass beads, 6 mm

1 pale pink glass bell flower, 12 x 18 mm

16 creamy pink glass faceted beads, 4 mm

8 cranberry glass barrel beads, 5 x 7 mm

7 large pink flower-shaped glass beads, 12 to 16 mm

34-inch (86.4 cm) length of drawn cable chain, 3 mm

38 head pins, 1 inch (2.5 cm)

20-inch (50.8 cm) length of cable chain, 3 mm

22-inch (55.9 cm) length of cable chain, 4 mm

1 jump ring, 3 mm

3 jump rings, 8 mm

Spring ring clasp, 12 mm

Tools

2 pairs of needle-nose pliers

Wire cutters

Instructions

1. To make the innermost strand, cut 16 inches (40.6 cm) of drawn cable chain. Thread one eggshell-colored bead onto each of seven head pins; attach these to the chain, starting at the center and making your way out on either side, skipping every two links. Cut off any extra wire from the head pins.

2. To make the next strand, use the remaining 18 inches (45.7 cm) of drawn cable chain. Use a head pin to attach the bell flower to the center of it. Again using head pins, attach six faceted 4-mm beads to each side of the bell flower. Where the head pins are too long, cut off any extra wire.

3. For the third strand, use the 20 inches (50.8 cm) of 3-mm cable chain. Attach six of the barrel beads, dangling from head pins and centered along the chain, skipping 10 links between each bead. Cut off any extra head pin wire.

4. Use the 4-mm cable chain for the outermost strand. Attach the remaining beads to it using head pins; use the four leftover faceted beads as stamens for the four largest flower-shaped beads. (Do this by first threading a faceted bead on a head pin, then the flower-shaped bead; finally, attach the pair to the chain.) Cut off the extra wire from the head pins.

5. Catch one end of all four strands in the 3-mm jump ring; before closing the ring, attach one side of the clasp.

6. Thread the four loose ends of the strands in an 8-mm jump ring. Close the jump ring, then link two more jump rings to it to make an extension chain. Attach the third jump ring to the other end of the clasp.

steel moons

This elegant design has a playful side. What makes it so much fun is the way your eyes move rhythmically over the beads.

Designer: Brenda Schweder

Finished size: Necklace, 16 inches (40.6 cm) with three pendants, each ¾ x ¾ inch (1.9 x 1.9 cm)

Materials

23-inch (58.4 cm) length of steel wire, 16 gauge

9-inch (22.9 cm) length of steel wire, 24 gauge

3 ivory shell pearls, 12 mm

Clasp of your choice

Tools

Heavy-duty cutters

Tape measure

Mandrel, ⅝ inch (1.6 cm)

Round-nose pliers

Flat-nose pliers

Hammer and block

Large round-nose pliers or forming pliers

Steel wool

Sealing wax and rag

Instructions

1. Use the heavy-duty cutters to cut three lengths of the 16-gauge wire, each 7½ inches (19.1 cm). Bend the center of each length around a ⅝-inch (1.6 cm) mandrel, making a complete circle.

2. With the smallest part of the round-nose pliers, form a plain loop at both ends of each wire length. Use the flat-nose pliers to orient the loops perpendicular to two of the wires.

3. Use your fingers to curve each wire length to follow the curvature of a 6-inch (15.2 cm) circle. Texture each wire with a steel hammer.

4. Cut three lengths of 24-gauge wire, each 3 inches (7.6 cm). Thread and center a pearl on each length. Fit the threaded pearl into the circle formed in step 1, and wrap the ends of the wire around the center top and center bottom of the circle. Use flat-nose pliers to completely wrap the 24-gauge wire around the 16-gauge wire.

5. Cut two lengths of 16-gauge wire, each 3 inches (7.6 cm). Bend a ⅜-inch (9.5 mm) plain loop at the ends of both lengths with large round-nose pliers or forming pliers. Use flat-nose pliers to bend the end of one loop into a straight section ¼ inch (6 mm) long, leaving an opening in the loop. Use round-nose pliers to bend plain loops at the opposite ends of each wire. Use your fingers to gently curve each wire. Texture each wire with a steel hammer.

6. Lay out the necklace with the perpendicular-looped lengths at each side, the parallel-looped lengths at the bottom, and the clasp halves at the top. Use chain-nose and flat-nose pliers to connect the loops.

7. Gently rub the wire with steel wool and seal it with wax.

carla

Ignore your to-do list as you wear this necklace, sipping coffee for hours with a friend. The striking design features an unusual color combination, and the pretty toggle is placed near the front to show it off.

Designer: Cynthia Deis

Finished size: 16 inches (40.6 cm) long

Materials

1 antiqued brass dapped square filigree cross, 50 mm

1 antiqued brass filigree ring, 32 mm

1 antiqued brass filigree spacer bar, 10 x 30 mm

1 rust, green, blue, and pink flat round cloisonné bead, 42 mm

8 purple vintage swirled diamond glass beads, 15 mm

7 rust knot vintage glass beads, 12 mm

1 rust seed bead, size 6°

1 antiqued brass 20-gauge head pin, 1 inch (2.5 cm)

2 antiqued brass oval jump rings, 4 x 5 mm

6 antiqued brass square jump rings, 9 mm

15-inch (38.1 cm) length of antiqued brass chain, 5 x 6 mm

24-inch (61 cm) length of gunmetal 20-gauge craft wire

Tools

Wire cutters

Chain-nose pliers

Round-nose pliers

Instructions

1. Cut the chain in one 14-inch (35.6 cm) length. Set this and the remaining 1-inch (2.5 cm) piece of chain aside.

2. Set the cloisonné bead on the back of the cross filigree, right in the center. Decide where the points of the cross will bend up and over the bead. It may be useful to sketch the pattern of the filigree and note the bend points on the sketch while working.

3. Use your fingers to gently bend the points of the filigree up to form right angles. Set the bead inside the filigree and continue to bend each point over the bead (figure 1).

    fig. 1

    Use chain-nose pliers to flatten the points down onto the bead. Take care not to scratch the bead's surface with the pliers. *Note:* If the bead is loose, use chain-nose pliers to carefully tighten the fit, working slowly from side point to side point—not clockwise. To create an even setting, make many small adjustments rather than a few large ones. Set the pendant aside.

4. Place the spacer bar on top of the filigree ring. Note the points where the bar overlaps the ring. Use chain-nose pliers to make a 45° bend at one of the points. Repeat to make a matching bend at the other end of the spacer bar (figure 2).

    fig. 2

5. Slip the seed bead on the head pin. Pass the head pin through the spacer bar's center hole from front to back. Trim the head pin to ⅜ inch (9 mm) and form a simple loop to secure the bead (figure 3). Use a square jump ring to attach the loop on the back of the spacer bar to the end link of the 1-inch (2.5 cm) piece of chain. Set the toggle bar aside.

    fig. 3

6. Cut a 1½-inch (3.8 cm) length of wire and form a simple loop at one end. Slide on one purple bead and form a simple loop to secure it. Repeat to create one-bead links with all the purple and rust beads.

fig. 4

fig. 5

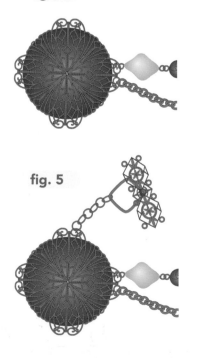

7. Attach the end of one purple bead link to the end of one rust bead link. Continue, connecting all the links to make an alternating-bead chain.

8. Connect an end loop of the bead chain to a side loop on the pendant. Use an oval jump ring to attach the end of the 14-inch (35.6 cm) piece of chain to the pendant's adjacent side loop (figure 4).

9. Use a square jump ring to connect the open ends of the bead-link chain and the 14-inch (35.6 cm) piece of chain to the filigree ring.

10. Move clockwise around the back of the pendant from the chains already placed. Note the next loop and use an oval jump ring to connect the toggle-bar chain to that loop (figure 5).

11. Open a square jump ring and lay the bead-link chain inside it between the third and fourth links. Lay the adjacent metal chain inside, too. Close the ring. Repeat with the remaining square jump rings, placing one square jump ring between each group of three bead links. Take care to loop the jump ring around the bead-link and metal chains, not through the chains.

chui

A bright mix of shapes and textures abounds in this African-inspired creation, which is named after the Swahili word for "leopard." The chain, made from hand-made jump rings, has just the right visual weight to complement its spiraled-wire pendants.

Designer: Andrea L. McLester

Finished size: 20 inches (50.8 cm) long

Materials

6 brown glass seed beads

6 sterling silver saucer-shaped beads, 5 mm

3 vintage red glass spacers, 4 mm

1 lampworked cylinder bead, ¾ inch (1.9 cm) long

2 palm-wood bicone beads, each ½ x ⅞ inch (1.3 x 2.2 cm) long

2 lampworked cylinder beads, ⅝ inch (1.6 cm) long

2 round mother-of-pearl beads, 8 mm

15-foot (4.6 m) length of 16-gauge dead-soft sterling silver wire

5-foot (1.5 m) length of 20-gauge dead-soft sterling silver wire

1 sterling silver toggle clasp

Tools

2 pairs of needle-nose pliers with nonserrated or plastic-coated jaws

¼-inch (0.6 cm) dowel or similar object to use as a mandrel

Tape measure

Wire cutters

2 pairs of round-nose pliers

Flat-nose pliers

Note: Adjust the length of the necklace if desired; it takes six jump rings, made from 16-gauge wire on a ¼-inch (0.6 cm) dowel, to make 1 inch (2.5 cm) of chain.

Instructions

1. To make a handmade chain, make a coil roughly 3 inches (7.6 cm) long on the dowel with the 16-gauge wire. Remove the coil and use wire cutters to cut 116 rings from the coil's length.

2. Using the needle-nose pliers, close half the rings.

3. Thread one open ring through two closed ones.

4. Use an open ring to join a closed ring to one end of the short bit of chain you made in step 3. Close the open ring. Repeat this process until you've used all but two of your rings. Use the final two rings to attach your toggle clasp to the ends of the chain.

5. Use wire cutters to cut ten 6-inch (15.2 cm) pieces of 20-gauge wire. Make 10 spiral head pins; four full turns should be sufficient. These will be used to make beaded pendants.

6. Thread one seed bead, one silver saucer, one red spacer, another saucer, and another seed bead onto a spiral head pin. Using round-nose pliers, make a small loop at the top of this bead that is perpendicular to the spiral. Trim any excess wire. Thread the small loop onto the outermost wrap of another spiral head pin. You may need to loosen the last wrap a bit so the pendant can hang properly from it. Add the ¾-inch (1.9 cm) cylinder bead to this second spiral head pin. Make a loop at the top of this bead and trim any excess wire. Attach this jointed pendant to the center link in your chain, carefully opening the loop in the same way you would a jump ring.

7. Cut a 6-inch (15.2 cm) piece of 16-gauge wire. Create a large spiral on one end, turning it three times. Thread the spiral through the second link from the center pendant and make another small spiral at the top, turning this spiral one and a half turns in the direction opposite that of the large spiral. To make it more visually interesting, use your thumb and forefinger to make the straight portion of the wire slightly wavy, until this short pendant is 1¾ inches (4.4 cm) long. Make another wavy wire piece for the other side of the center pendant.

8. Make two more beaded pendants as described in step 6, using bicone beads instead of cylinders. Attach them to the chain, on either side of the wavy wire pendants, skipping a link between them.

9. Make and attach two more wavy wire pendants, as you did in step 7. If necessary, make additional turns to the lower spiral so that it's approximately 1¼ inches (3.2 cm) long.

10. Thread one of the smaller cylinder beads onto a spiral head pin. Make a loop at the top of the bead. Repeat to make a second pendant. Attach the small loops to the chains as before.

11. Make another pair of wavy wire spirals from 6-inch (15.2 cm) pieces of 16-gauge wire, turning them each four times. Attach them as before, closing with a small spiral at the top. These pendants should be approximately 1 inch (2.5 cm) long. If necessary, make additional turns to the lower spiral to achieve this length.

12. Thread one mother-of-pearl bead onto each of the last two spiral head pins. Make loops at the tops of the beads and attach these outermost pendants to the chain.

forever
yours

The most fragile of mementos can become long-lasting treasures
with the clever use of microscope slides and a foiling technique.

Designer: Linda Larsen

Finished size: 16 inches (40.6 cm) long

Materials

3 crystal beads (flat-back), 4 mm

2 sterling silver rondelle spacers, 4 mm

Aqua faceted crystals (round), 9 mm

5 aqua bicone crystals, 6 mm

5 turquoise nuggets, 5 to 10 mm

5 turquoise cushion beads, 6 mm

Flat, round turquoise nugget, 22 mm

Turquoise pendant nugget, 12 mm

4 brass charms, 25 mm

Brass locket, 18 mm

Found objects: brass zipper pull, piece of old tin can, rusted snap, vintage jewelry parts, and mother-of-pearl wristwatch face and button

Dried hydrangea petal

Postage stamp

Brass locket, 16 mm

16 sterling silver jump rings, 6 mm

8 sterling silver jump rings, 13 mm

Sterling silver jump ring, 13 mm, for the button, wristwatch face, and other objects to be edged with foil

4 ball-end head pins, 2 inches (5 cm)

36-inch (90 cm) length of 22-gauge sterling silver wire

16-inch (40.6 cm) length of sterling silver chain necklace with closure, 18 mm

(Continued on next page)

Instructions

1. Age all of the brass pieces with the patina, according to the manufacturer's instructions. Glue the flat-back crystals to unexpected places on any of the pieces, such as the front and back of the oval brass locket and the front of the zipper pull. Glue the scrap of fabric to one side of the large locket, and glue a charm on top of the fabric.

2. Set aside the found objects with holes near the top. These holes can be used to add the pieces to chain in a later step. The rest will need to be wired with organic or embellished loops. To make an organic loop, start by cutting the wire for a wrapped loop 4 to 6 inches (10.2 to 15.2 cm) longer than usual. Make the loop and then loosely wrap it, pushing down on the coil with your thumb as you wrap to make it chubby. You can also handle the wire like thread by using a buttonhole stitch to sew around a loop.

3. Don the safety glasses. Score the microscope slide with the glass cutter by running a line at the place you want to cut it to fit the dried and pressed hydrangea petal. Do not continue the score line to the edges. Gently snap the pieces apart by holding the slide on each side of the scored line with your fingers.

Designer's Tips

You can use more than one type of wire to attach your charms. This will add subtle—yet interesting—visual texture to your finished piece. Keep in mind that the wire must be strong enough to withstand the charm's movement when the necklace is worn. You might want to double the loops if you have any doubts about a wire's strength.

Some patina solutions work best if the pieces are left to dry in the sunshine, because the heat helps the chemicals do their job more efficiently.

To give your piece more movement, attach some dangles or charms with large jump rings. These also act as an additional design element when evenly spaced along the chain.

Materials (continued)

18-inch (45.7 cm) length of sterling silver chain, 1.5 mm

Patina solution for metallic surfaces

Craft glue

1-inch (2.5 cm) square of fabric

2 microscope glass slides

Roll of ¼-inch silver-back copper foil tape, 6 mm

Flux and applicator brush

Lead-free solder

Tools

2 pairs of chain-nose pliers

Round-nose pliers

Wire cutters

Safety glasses

Glass cutter

Soldering iron

Flux applicator brush

Chasing hammer

4. Place the petal between the two pieces of glass. Join the layers by running the foil tape around the edges. Overlap the beginning and end ¼ inch (6 mm). Press the lengthwise edges of the foil tape over the edges of the glass surfaces. Burnish the foil with your thumbnail. Apply the flux. Paint the solder over the tape with the soldering iron. Solder a large jump ring to the top. In the same manner, encase the stamp. Also edge and attach a large jump ring to other found objects, such as the mother-of-pearl button and wristwatch face.

5. Thread the rondelle spacer and large crystal onto a head pin, and complete the dangle with a wrapped loop. Make three of the small bicones into individual dangles using a head pin with a wrapped loop at the top of each one.

6. Secure the small locket to a piece of wire with a wrapped loop. Thread each of the remaining bicones onto separate head pins. Twist the three wire ends together and handle them as a single strand in order to make one wrapped loop (figure 1). Use this same process to create a dangle using three turquoise cushions.

fig. 1

7. Thread a vintage jewelry piece and a charm onto a small jump ring, to make a single charm.

8. Place each large jump ring on a bench block and gently hammer the bottom to slightly flatten them.

9. Select the five largest pieces from the found objects, lockets, and jewelry items. Attach these, evenly spaced, along the center third of the chain, using a large jump ring for each one. Use smaller jump rings to attach all of the remaining lockets and dangles—also evenly spaced—along the center third of the chain.

10. Thread a 2-inch (5.1 cm) piece of wire through a small nugget, and finish with a wrapped loop. Attach this to one end of the necklace chain, just beyond the last attached charm, using a jump ring. Make a wrapped loop at the opposite end of the nugget, at the same time attaching it to the end of the tiny chain. Wrap and loop the chain through the larger

necklace links around the charms, cutting the chain to insert nuggets with wrapped loops as needed to give the necklace a cohesive appearance. (Treat the remaining two turquoise cushions as a single nugget by threading them onto a wire with a rondelle spacer in between.)

11. If desired, secure the fine chain at strategic points along the necklace by threading the chain through an existing jump ring, or attach a jump ring to a necklace link for this purpose. Use another nugget with wrapped loops to secure the opposite end of the fine chain to a link beyond the last charm at the opposite end of the necklace (figure 2).

fig. 2

simply charming

If charms can be sentimental or meaningful, why not beads? All you intrepid bead lovers have, no doubt, collected some bright and fanciful ones in your travels. This necklace gives you a stylish way to use them so you can recall favorite times and places.

Designer: Molly Dingledine

Finished size: 30 inches (76.2 cm) long

Materials

36 beads—anything goes, as long as it has a hole in it— vintage glass, shell, wood, metal, etc.

Medium- to large-link chain

36 head pins

Tools

Round-nose pliers

Wire cutters

Liver of sulphur

Instructions

1. Use the liver of sulphur to oxidize the chain and head pins. This design retains most of the oxidation on the chain to achieve a darker finish that offsets the brightness of the beads.

2. String the beads on the head pins as desired. Using the round-nose pliers, make wrapped loops with one or two wraps for attaching beads that will dangle from the links of chain.

3. Cut the tops off some head pins and string one bead on each. Make wrapped loops at both ends of the bead so you can open the links of the chain and attach the beads to them. Space these beads randomly or evenly to your liking.

4. Have fun attaching beads all the way around the chain until you've used them all. Then, voilà my dear, it's time to go out and turn on the charm.

waves of pearls

Green, which was quite fashionable during the Victorian era, is featured in this dramatic design. You'll find this color comes in an incredible array of shades, including emerald, avocado, and aventurine.

Designers: Marty Stevens-Heebner and Christine Calla

Finished size: 15½ inches (39.4 cm) long

Materials

55 head pins

92 round freshwater pearls, 6 mm

64 bicone crystal AB beads, 4 mm

36 bicone crystal beads, 6 mm

36-inch (91.4 cm) length of 24-gauge gold wire

1-inch (2.5 cm) length of gold chain

1 jump ring

Clasp

Tools

2 pairs of round-nose pliers

Needle-nose pliers

Wire cutters

Tape measure

Instructions

1. Slide a freshwater pearl onto onc of the head pins, then add a 4-mm bicone. Grasp the end of the head pin with the round-nose pliers, and make a small loop in the wire. Wrap the remaining wire around the pin two to three times between the bottom of the loop and the top of the bead using the needle-nose pliers. Trim any excess wire, then repeat this step 18 more times.

2. Thread a 4-mm bicone bead onto one of the head pins, then add two pearls and a 6-mm bicone. Follow the procedure in step 1 to form a wrapped loop at the top. Repeat this step 18 more times.

3. Slide a 6-mm bicone onto a head pin, followed by two 4-mm bicones. Form a loop in the end of the head pin with the round-nose pliers, then slide one of the head pins from step 2 onto this loop. Wrap any remaining wire beneath the bottom of the loop using the needle-nose pliers, and trim away any excess wire. Repeat this step 9 more times.

4. Thread a 6-mm crystal bead onto another head pin, then add a 4-mm bicone bead. Form a loop in the end of the head pin with the round-nose pliers, slide one of the head pins from step 2 onto this loop, and wrap any remaining wire beneath the bottom of the loop using the needle-nose pliers. Trim any excess wire with the wire cutters, then repeat this step 9 more times.

5. Cut a 24-inch (61 cm) piece of the 24-gauge wire with the wire cutters. Grasp one end of the wire with the round-nose pliers, and follow the procedure in step 1 to create a wrapped loop.

6. Slide a pearl onto this wire. Thread the wire through the loop of one of the head pins from step 1, then add another pearl. Now add a head pin from step 3 by looping the 24-gauge wire once between the two pearls on the head pin and pulling it taut. Repeat this step, except replace the head pin from step 3 with a head pin from step 4.

7. Repeat step 6 three more times. Cut a 1-inch (2.5 cm) piece of the gold chain and a 1½-inch (3.8 cm) piece of the 24-gauge wire. Grasp the wire ½ inch (1.3 cm) from one end with the round-nose pliers, and form a small loop. Wrap the remaining wire two to three times beneath this loop using the needle-nose pliers. Trim any extra wire.

8. Slide a pearl and then a 4-mm bicone onto the wire. Using the round-nose pliers, form a loop in the other end of the wire. Slip one end of the chain onto this loop, then wrap the remaining wire two to three times between the loop and the beads with the needle-nose pliers. Trim any extra wire.

9. Slide a 4-mm bicone onto a head pin, then add two pearls and a 6-mm bicone. Grasp the end of the head pin with the round-nose pliers, and form a small loop. Slip this loop through the other end of the chain length. Wrap the remaining wire around the pin two to three times between the bottom of the loop and the top of the bead, using the needle-nose pliers, and trim any excess wire.

10. Thread the piece from step 9 onto the necklace via the top loop. Then repeat step 6 four additional times.

11. Grasp one end of the wire with the round-nose pliers, and form a small loop. Wrap the remaining wire around the pin two to three times between the bottom of the loop and the top of the bead, using the needle-nose pliers. Trim any excess wire.

12. Open one of the jump rings, slip it through the loop at one end of the necklace, and close the ring. Then open the jump ring attached to the clasp, slide it through the wire loop at the opposite end of the necklace, and close the ring. If you like, you can add an extender to the back of the necklace.

lucille

Colorful and fun, this necklace is off-balance and quirky. The mixed beads and asymmetrical filigree look random, but they're carefully balanced to hang evenly on your neck.

Designer: Cynthia Deis

Finished size: 24 inches (61 cm) long

Materials

3 raw brass filigree pinwheels, 48 mm

97 assorted red glass beads, 3 to 9 mm

27 antiqued brass 20-gauge head pins, 1 inch (2.5 cm)

34-inch (86.4 cm) length of antiqued brass chain, 5 x 6 mm

10-inch (25.4 cm) length of gunmetal 20-gauge craft wire

Bright red enamel spray paint

Clear enamel spray paint

Newsprint or scrap cardboard

Tools

Wire cutters

Chain-nose pliers

Round-nose pliers

Note

The project shown was created using many vintage beads, so it may be impossible to make an exact duplicate. Instead, use orphan beads from your bead stash in your favorite color and work with them. Paint the filigree to match your beads.

Instructions

1. Cut the chain into three pieces: one 9-inch (22.9 cm), one 11-inch (27.9 cm), and one 14-inch (35.6 cm) length. Set aside.

2. Clean the pinwheels so they're free of lint or dust. Set aside.

3. Working in a well-ventilated area, set a few sheets of newsprint or scrap cardboard down to protect your work surface. Use red paint to spray a thin coat on the front of the pinwheels. Allow to dry for 60 to 90 minutes. Spray on a second coat and let dry again. Flip the pinwheels over and spray the back sides, allowing to dry for 60 to 90 minutes. Turn the pinwheels over and spray a thin, clear coat of enamel; allow to dry for at least 60 to 90 minutes. Spray another clear coat on the front, and at least one on the back. Allow the finished pieces to dry for 24 hours so the paint can cure.

4. Lay out the necklace design. Start by placing the pinwheels so there are two pieces on the left side and one piece on the right. Lay the chain pieces so the 11-inch (27.9 cm) length is at the top of the necklace, the 14-inch (35.6 cm) length is at the bottom, and the 9-inch (22.9-cm) length crosses between the top two pinwheels (figure 1).

fig. 1

5. Spend some time with the accent beads, experimenting with placement. The beads will attach to the chain in dangles, so group the smaller beads in sets to create longer dangles, and let the larger beads stand on their own. Always keep the balance of bead color and size in mind. Place about two-thirds of the beads on the left side of the necklace, the remaining beads mainly on the right side. Set aside some beads to connect the pinwheels to the chains.

6. Cut a length of wire as long as your bead, or bead set, plus ¾ inch (1.9 cm). Form a simple loop at one end, slip on the bead(s), and form another simple loop to secure. Repeat to make at least seven bead links of different sizes.

7. Imagine the pinwheel on the right side of the necklace as a clock face. Connect bead links to the pinwheel: one at twelve o'clock, one at five o'clock, and one at seven o'clock.

8. Repeat the placement in step 7 for the top pinwheel on the left side of the necklace, this time adding two links to the seven o'clock position. Connect the two pinwheels on the necklace's left side with the seven o'clock links. Attach two links to the bottom pinwheel's six o'clock position (figure 2).

9. Use the bead links at the top left and top right of the pinwheels to attach the 14-inch (35.6 cm) piece of chain. Use the bead link at the bottom left pinwheel's five o'clock position to attach the 11-inch (27.9 cm) piece of chain to the right-side pinwheel's seven o'clock position.

10. Use the remaining attached bead links to add the 9-inch (22.9 cm) piece of chain across the middle of the necklace.

11. Slide the remaining beads onto head pins, singly or in groups of two to five. Secure the beads with a simple loop to make dangles. Attach the dangles to the 11-inch (27.9 cm) and 9-inch (22.9 cm) chain links (figure 3). Spend some time balancing the dangles as you work, noting the weight and size of the various beads and placing them in their best positions. The dangle placement is not only aesthetic but necessary to keep the necklace weighted properly.

12. Try on the necklace to see if you are pleased with the design. If necessary, move the dangles until you achieve the desired effect.

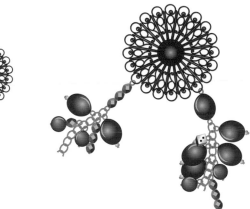

fig. 2   fig. 3

wisdom

Three inspirational words—Live, Love, Laugh—are stamped in polymer clay and highlighted with color and combined with wire-wrapped beads to make a charming necklace.

Designer: Patty Cox

Finished size: 24 inches (61 cm) long

Materials

48-inch (144.8 cm) length of 24-gauge gold wire

7 bead charms

30 or more assorted green glass beads

Translucent polymer clay

Alphabet rubber stamps

Green dye or paint

Gold spring ring clasp, 6 mm

Gold jump rings

Rubber stamps with words (Choose ones that make a deep impression.)

Wax paper

Spray gloss finish

20 eye pins

32 jump rings

Tools

Needle-nose pliers

Round-nose pliers

Rolling pin

Wire cutters

Instructions

Make Clay Charms

1. Soften the clay. Roll to ¼ inch (6 mm) thickness between the sheets of wax paper.

2. Press three of the bead charms into clay. Cover with wax paper. Roll over the clay and charms with rolling pin. Remove the clay-filled charms.

3. Cut three 3-inch (7.6 cm) pieces of gold wire. Insert a piece of wire through the side holes of each clay-filled charm.

4. Press a rubber stamp in each clay charm, making a deep impression.

5. Bake the charm-filled clay. Let cool.

6. Rub paint or dye into the crevices left by stamping in clay. Let dry.

7. Spray the charms with a gloss finish.

Make Wrapped Beads

8. See figures 1, 2, and 3. The instructions are for one bead. Repeat for succeeding beads.

9. Cut a 6-inch (15.2 cm) length of gold wire. Hold the wire 1 inch (2.5 cm) from the end with the round-nose pliers. Fold the wire over the round nose, forming a loop. Add a bead over both wires (figure 1).

10. Form a loop on other end of the wire next to the bead, using the round-nose pliers. Hold the loop with the pliers and wrap the wire tightly around the loop. (figure 2).

11. Continue spiraling the wire around the bead and end the wire tightly around the loop on the other end of the bead. Cut the wire tails (figure 3).

12. With the needle-nose pliers, grasp one wire wrap on the bead. Twist the needle-nose pliers to tighten the wire and form a decorative bend in the wire wrap.

Add Eye Pins to Unwrapped Beads

13. Thread each bead on an eye pin. Form a loop at the end of the eye pin.

14. Repeat for the remaining beads.

Add Beads to Charms

15. Pull out the wire from the charms.

16. Insert an eye pin into the side hole of one bead charm. Thread a bead on the eye pin, then thread the eye pin end through the other side hole of the bead charm. Form a loop at the end of the eye pin.

17. Repeat for the remaining charms.

Assemble

18. Connect all the beads and charms with jump rings, using the photo as a guide.

19. Attach the clasp at ends of the necklace.

fig. 1

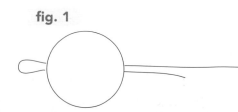

fig. 2

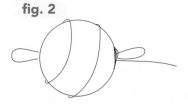

fig. 3

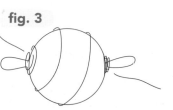

As long as you keep the scale of your dangles small and delicate, they don't have to be perfectly matched.

Designer: Kaari Meng

Finished size: 23 inches (58.4 cm) long

Materials

1 brass bezel, 7 x 10 mm

1 brass bezel, 10 x 14 mm

3 brass bezels, 6 x 8 mm

43-inch (1.1 m) length of brass cable chain, 3 mm

17-inch (43.2 cm) length of brass figaro chain, 9 mm

1 opal glass cabachon, 10 x 14 mm

1 opal glass cabachon, 6 x 8 mm

1 milk glass cabachon, 7 x 10 mm

2 speckled glass cabachons, 6 x 8 mm

4 brass charms

5 teal glass egg beads, 11 x 18 mm

20 white glass feather beads, 6 x 9 mm

6 blue glass leaves, 6 x 9 mm

31 brass head pins, 1 inch (2.5 cm)

2 brass jump rings, 10 mm

15 brass oval jump rings, 3 x 4 mm

1 brass spring ring clasp, 12 mm

Tools

Jeweler's glue

Needle-nose pliers

Wire cutters

Instructions

1. Glue the cabochons into their respective bezels; set aside to dry.

2. To make the first strand, locate the center link in the figaro chain. Thread a teal glass egg bead onto a head pin, then cut and loop directly onto the chain. Thread two more egg beads onto two head pins, and attach to either side, approximately 1¾ inches (4.4 cm) apart.

3. To make the second strand, use wire cutters to cut a piece of cable chain that measures 20 inches (50.8 cm) long. Next, thread the white glass feather beads onto head pins, then cut and loop them directly onto the 20-inch (50.8 cm) cable chain, ½ inch (1.3 cm) apart.

4. To make the third strand, find the center of the remaining 23-inch (58.4 cm) piece of cable chain and attach the 10 x 14-mm opal charm using an oval jump ring. Attach three blue glass leaves, two charms, and two speckled cabochons to either side of the opal using oval jump rings, leaving about ½ inch (1.3 cm) between each bead. Continue attaching leaves, charms, and cabochons to the opposite side of the chain to balance out the third strand.

5. Attach the clasp to the end of all three strands using a 10-mm jump ring. Attach the remaining 10-mm jump ring to the opposite end of all three strands of chain.

Designer's Tip

Chain extensions are great for making chokers into longer necklaces, lending versatility to any short necklace. Simply add an extension of chain—at least 3 inches (7.6 cm)—to the back of the necklace using a jump ring. You can also dangle an embellishment threaded onto a head pin off the end of the chain for a decorative touch. Another way to create an extension is to link four to five 5-mm jump rings together at the end of a necklace.

garland

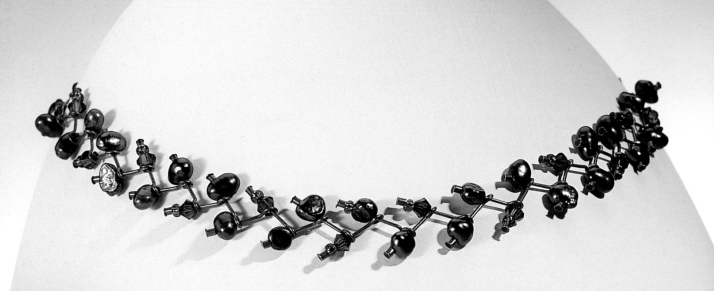

This nature-inspired necklace looks like a dainty chain of flowers
a wood fairy might fashion. Change the pearl, crystal, and metal
types, and you can evoke any season of the year.

Designer: Ellen Gerritse

Finished size: 16 inches (40.6 cm) long

Materials

46 brown half-round potato freshwater pearls, 6 mm

22 transparent brown crystal bicones, 4 mm

22 transparent topaz seed beads, size 11°

68 dark copper head pins, 1½ inches (3.8 cm)

68 dark copper crimp tubes, 2 x 2 mm

1 dark copper split ring, 5 mm

1 dark copper spring ring clasp, 8 mm

1-inch (2.5-cm) length of twisted oval link dark copper chain, 4 mm

Tools

Crimping pliers

Wire cutters

Flat-nose pliers

Round-nose pliers

Ruler or measuring tape

Instructions

1. Slide a crimp tube onto a head pin. Snug the tube next to the pin's head and crimp. String on a pearl. Make a 90° bend in the wire 4 mm from the top of the pearl. Form a simple loop starting at the bend. Open the loop and attach it to an end link on the chain. Set this chain extender aside.

2. String a crimp tube onto a head pin. Snug the tube up to the pin's head and crimp. Slide on a pearl. As in step 1, measure 4 mm from the top of the pearl, bend the wire 90°, and then make a simple loop. Finish the loop and attach it to the clasp. Set aside.

3. Slide a crimp tube onto a head pin. Push the tube snugly beside the pin's head and crimp. String on a pearl. As before, make a simple loop 4 mm from the top of the pearl. Open the loop and attach it to the head pin made in step 2, between the pearl and the clasp (figure 1). Set aside.

fig. 1

4. String a crimp tube onto a head pin. Snug the tube next to the pin's head and crimp. String on one seed bead and one crystal. Make a simple loop 4 mm from the top of the crystal. Open the loop and attach it to the head pin added in the previous step, between the bead and the simple loop.

5. Slide a crimp tube onto a head pin. Push the tube snugly next to the pin's head and crimp. String on a pearl. Make a simple loop 4 mm from the top of the crystal. Open the loop and attach it to the head pin added in the previous step, between the bead and the simple loop.

Designer's Tip

Marking the jaws of your flat-nose pliers to 4 mm will speed the process of making the necklace.

6. Repeat step 5.

7. Repeat steps 4 through 6 twenty times.

8. Repeat step 4. Set the necklace aside.

9. Cut the head off of a head pin. Make a simple loop at one end. Use the split ring to attach the loop and the open end of the chain. String on a crimp tube, snug it next to the loop, and crimp. String on a pearl and make a simple loop 4 mm from the first simple loop. Attach this loop to the head pin added in step 8, between the bead and the simple loop (figure 2).

fig. 2

year of the dragon

Whatever your Chinese zodiac sign is, wearing this necklace will bring you good fortune.

Designer: Jeannette Chiang Bardi

Finished Size: 17½ inches
(44.5 cm) long

Materials

30-inch (76.2 cm) length of 22-gauge
square half-hard gold-filled wire,
either 12/20 or 14/20

5 round cream-colored (natural) river
stone beads, 6 mm

5 round earth-tone (natural) picture
jasper beads, 6 mm

6 round gold Swarovski crystal pearls,
6 mm

5 round black Swarovski crystal pearls,
6 mm

3 diamond-shaped black imitation
cinnabar beads, 15 mm

Antique brass Chinese Zodiac
"protective talisman" coin drop,
30 x 23 mm

6-inch (15.2 cm) length of black
leather cord, 2 mm

4 gold-filled or gold-plated coil ends,
each 10.5 x 3 mm

Lobster clasp with ring,
12 x 5 x 2.5 mm

Tools

Ruler or tape measure

Wire cutters

Round-nose pliers

Flat-nose pliers

Scissors

Instructions

1. To make the bead/wire components, begin by cutting the gold-filled
   wire with the wire cutters into twenty-three 1-inch (2.5 cm) lengths and
   three 1½-inch (3.8 cm) lengths.

2. Take one of the 1-inch (2.5 cm) lengths of gold-filled wire, and using
   the round-nose pliers, bend ⅓ inch (8.5 mm) of the wire into a simple
   loop. Slip a 6-mm bead on the straight end of the wire. With the bead
   snug to the first loop, create a second loop on the other end of the bead,
   but leave the loop slightly open (see the steps in figure 1). Create a total
   of 21 bead/wire components out of the 6-mm beads, using the 1-inch
   (2.5 cm) lengths of gold-filled wire.

fig. 1

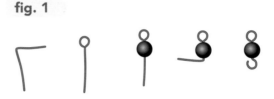

3. Using the same procedure as used when making the 6-mm bead/wire
   components, use the three 1½ inch (3.8 cm) lengths of gold-filled wire
   to create three cinnabar bead/wire components. Bend ½ inch (1.3 cm)
   of the wire for each loop on either side of the bead.

4. Set aside one gold pearl/wire component and one cinnabar bead/wire
   component to be used for the pendant.

5. With the remaining bead/wire components, create two 11-bead
   strands by linking together the 6-mm bead/wire components made
   in steps 2 and 3, using the flat-nose pliers to close each link securely.
   Alternate the bead types, and attach a cinnabar bead as the ninth
   bead/wire component in each strand. This will make the two sides of
   the necklace.

6. To create the pendant, begin by linking the remaining gold/pearl wire component to one end of the remaining cinnabar bead. On the other side of the gold/pearl wire component, link the Chinese coin.

7. Bring the ends of the two necklace strands, with the cinnabar beads toward the bottom, and attach the bottom two links together with the cinnabar end of the pendant.

8. To make and connect the cord ends, begin by cutting two 3-inch (7.6 cm) lengths of leather cord.

9. Bend both ends of each cord back ½ inch (1.3 cm). Use the flat-nose pliers to squeeze the folded end so that it will keep its shape and slip more easily into a coil end, leaving a leather loop. Twist gently to insert the coil end over the leather loop (top of figure 2). Secure the coil by squeezing the first and last loop of the coil onto the cord. Again use the flat-nose pliers (bottom of figure 2). Repeat for the other three ends.

fig. 2

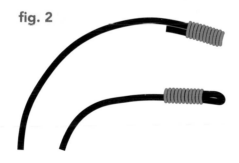

10. Use the remaining two 1-inch (2.5 cm) lengths of gold-filled wire to create two links, using the same procedure referenced in step 2 (only without the beads). Slip the open end of one of the links through the leather loop at the end of each cord and close to secure. Attach half of the lobster claw clasp to one of the links. Attach the lobster claw ring to a link on the other cord. Finally, link the necklace to the other ends of the cord.

snow

Combine a flurry of pearls with sterling silver hammered disks and hoops to make a free-flowing necklace with ever-changing shapes and textures.

Designer: Valérie MacCarthy

Finished size: 17½ inches (44.5 cm) long

Materials

34 pearls disks, some 10 mm and some 12 mm

14 sterling silver hammered disks, 12 mm

13 sterling silver hammered hoops, 15 mm

1 sterling silver lobster clasp

80-inch (203.2 cm) length of sterling silver chain, 2.5 mm

160-inch (406.4 cm) length of sterling silver 24-gauge wire

4-inch (12.7 cm) length of sterling silver 22-gauge wire

Tools

Chain-nose pliers

Round-nose pliers

Wire cutters

Large rubberized round-nose pliers

Ruler

Instructions

1. Cut the chain into ½-inch (1.3 cm) and 1½-inch (3.8 cm) segments.

2. Using the round-nose pliers, make a loop in the 24-gauge wire about ¾ inch (1.9 cm) from the end. Slide this loop onto the chain. Hold the wire with the chain-nose pliers and twist the wires around to secure. Cut off the shorter wire end.

3. Slide one 10- or 12-mm pearl onto the wire. Bend the wire 45°. Hold the wire with the round-nose pliers and loop the wire around.

4. Now slide a new chain end onto this loop. Hold the loop with the round-nose pliers and wrap the wire around to secure. Cut off the excess wire.

5. Select a sterling silver hoop. Slide the 24-gauge wire through the hoop. Bend the wire so that it surrounds the hoop tightly and bend it again so that the wires cross; twist the wire ends together and cut off the shorter wire end. Using the round-nose pliers, loop the wire around and slide it through the final link in the chain.

6. Hold the wire loop with the chain-nose pliers and wrap the wire around the twist you made in step 5 to secure (figure 1). Cut off the excess wire.

fig. 1

7. Attach a new piece of chain onto the opposite side of the hoop, using the same twisted wire loop link technique from steps 5 and 6.

8. Make a new loop in the wire about ¾ inch (1.9 cm) from the end and place it onto the end of the new piece of chain. Hold this loop with the chain-nose pliers and twist the wires around to secure. Cut off the shorter wire end. This time, slide on perhaps one 10-mm disk pearl, one 12-mm disk pearl, and one 10-mm disk pearl. Bend the wire 45°, and loop it around using the round-nose pliers. Place it onto a new piece of chain. Hold the loop with the chain-nose pliers. Wrap the wire around to secure and cut off the excess.

9. Select one of the silver disks and slide the wire through one of its holes. Bend the wire until both ends are crossed tightly. Twist the wires together and cut off the shorter wire end. Wrap the wire around using the round-nose pliers and slide it through the final link in the chain. Hold the loop with the chain-nose pliers and wrap the wire around the twist you just made to secure (figure 2). Cut off the excess wire.

fig. 2

10. Attach another wire loop, as in step 9, to the other side of this silver disk and follow with another piece of chain.

11. Continue adding on segments as described above in steps 2 through 10, connecting them with twisted wire loop links. The chain segments should alternate between ½ inch (1.3 cm) and 1½ inches (3.8 cm). Switch from pearls to silver hoops or disks as you go along. Feel free to use one, two, or three pearls at a time, depending on your preference.

12. As the strand reaches 14 inches (35.6 cm) in length, end the strand with a piece of chain. Set it aside and begin a new strand. Make a total of five 14-inch (35.6 cm) strands, each beginning and ending with a piece of chain.

13. After completing all five strands, join them onto a single loop. Using the round-nose pliers, hold the 22-gauge wire about ¾ inch (1.9 cm) from the end and loop the wire around. Place the end links of all five strands onto this loop. Hold the loop with the chain-nose pliers and twist the wire around to secure. Cut off the shorter wire end.

14. Using the round-nose pliers, make a new loop in the wire and slide the clasp onto this loop. Hold the loop with the chain-nose pliers and wrap the wire around the twist you made in step 13. Cut off the excess wire.

15. Using the round-nose pliers, make a new loop in the 22-gauge wire and slide the opposite end links of the five strands onto this loop. (Before placing the strands onto the loop, let them all hang down to make sure they are not tangled or twisted.)

16. After all five strands are on the loop, hold this loop with the chain-nose pliers and twist the wires around to secure. Cut off the shorter wire end.

17. Using the rubberized round-nose pliers, wrap the wire around to make a large loop. Grip this loop with the rubberized pliers and wrap the wire around the twist you made in step 16. Cut off the excess wire.

vintage

Made almost exclusively from found components, this necklace recalls a past aesthetic. Look for beads that resemble the ones used here. This will give you an opportunity to indulge in a bead lover's favorite pastime—the thrill of the hunt.

Designer: Chris Franchetti Michaels

Finished size: 34 inches (86.4 cm) long with a 6-inch (15 cm) fringe

Materials

5 green vintage pressed-glass tablet beads with floral motif

4 opaque, light green vintage faceted-glass rounds

Fire-polished faceted-glass beads:
    5 green
    5 dark topaz

6 brown leopard-swirl glass rondelles

1 jade green vintage molded-glass Buddha bead

13 amber-colored vintage glass beads in long, rounded-side tablets

5 citrus-colored Mexican lampworked glass beads in organic shapes

3 brass hourglass tubes

1 antique-brass finish bulldog charm

3-foot (0.9 m) length of vintage brass filigree-bead chain

Ornate brass-plated pewter toggle

14½-foot (4.4m) length of 20-gauge round brass wire

Bead board

Tools

Wire cutters

Round-nose pliers

Smooth-jaw chain-nose pliers

Flat-nose pliers

Chasing hammer and jeweler's block

Ruler

Instructions

1. Choose a mix of bead colors, shapes, and textures, then lay them on a bead board. Select beads that will go together to make linked groupings. For example, in this necklace three amber-colored tablet beads make one grouping; an opaque green faceted-glass round, a small green faceted-glass bead, and a medium brown, leopard-swirl rondelle make another; and so on.

2. Cut lengths of wire that are long enough to make wrapped loops on either side of each bead. Working in bead groupings, string each bead in the group on a length of wire, then use the round-nose pliers to make wrapped loops for attaching the beads together as you work.

3. Divide the chain you're using into varying lengths. The purchased vintage chain is made from a series of small filigree balls strung on wire connected by simple loops. The loops were unsoldered, making it easy to divide the chain using chain-nose pliers.

4. Link the bead groupings to the chain lengths as desired. Since the design is a double necklace—a choker within a longer rope length—you'll make the choker and the two sides separately before attaching them. Make two equal lengths, each approximately 17 inches (43.2 cm) long, and one shorter length for the choker approximately 15 inches (38.1 cm) long. It's important that each length begins and ends with chain.

5. Make four short bead-and-chain lengths for the tassels. Vary the lengths for more interest. Include the bulldog charm on one of the lengths.

6. Use the round-nose pliers and wire to make two double-wrapped loops. Attach the loops, each to an end of one of the longer lengths, then attach the choker to the same loops. Next, attach the bar side of the toggle to one of the double loops, and the ring side to the other.

7. Join the necklace and attach the tassels with a simple figure-eight loop. To make it, use the widest part of the round-nose pliers to make one large loop in a length of wire. Wrap the tail around the base of the loop a few times. Then make another loop from the tail on the other side of the wrapping (at this point, it will look like a figure eight). To finish, wrap the remaining tail at the base of the second loop around the first wrapping. Attach the ends of the necklace to one loop and the beaded tassels to the other.

8. A flattened coil adds a finishing touch to the end of each tassel. To make one, use the round-nose pliers to make a tiny loop at the end of a length of wire, then use the flat-nose pliers to coil wire around the loop a few times. Lay the coil on the jeweler's block and use a chasing hammer to flatten it. String a bead on the wire, make a wrapped loop, and attach it to the end of the tassel. Repeat for the other tassels.

peridot fairy

Peridot, which is found in meteorites, is believed by some to bring good luck. Said to bring understanding of purpose, it aids in transforming physical work into material abundance. In this necklace, peridot chips are combined with green glass leaf beads and liquid silver beads and accented with a pewter fairy.

Designer: Patty Cox

Finished size: 22 inches (55.9 cm) long

Materials

28-inch (71.1 cm) strand of peridot bead chips

23 liquid silver beads, 1.5 x 6 mm

10 green glass leaf beads

1 pewter fairy with crystal pendant

3 lime round beads, 6/0 (E beads)

1 heart toggle clasp

2 silver crimp beads

Beading wire, .014 inch

Tools

Wire cutters

Crimping tool

Instructions

1. Cut two 28-inch (71.1 cm) lengths of beading wire. Thread a crimp bead onto both wires. Thread the wires through one side of the toggle clasp, then back through the crimp bead, leaving 1-inch (2.5 cm) tails.

2. Thread a liquid silver bead over both wires and tails. Separate the wires.

3. On each wire, thread 1 inch (2.5 cm) of peridot bead chips. Bring the wire ends together.

4. Thread a liquid silver bead, leaf bead, and another liquid silver bead on both wires. Separate the wires.

5. Thread 1 inch (2.5 cm) of peridot bead chips on each wire. Bring the wire ends together.

6. Repeat steps 2 and 3 four times. Separate the wires. Add a 1-inch (2.5 cm) length of peridot bead chips on each wire. Bring the wire ends together. Thread a liquid silver bead on both wires.

7. On the lower wire, thread three green 6/0 round beads. Bring the wire through the pendant loop, then back through the three green 6/0 beads. Bring both wire ends together. Thread a liquid silver bead on both wires.

8. Follow steps 3 through 6 for the second half of the necklace.

9. Bring the ends of the wires together. Thread a liquid silver bead and a crimp bead on both wires. Thread the wires through the other side of the toggle clasp, then back through the crimp bead and liquid silver bead. Pull the wires taut. Crimp the bead, and cut the wire tails.

revelry

This colorful necklace with a South-of-the-Border
sensibility makes a simple outfit ready for a party.

Designer: Patty Cox

Finished size: 26 inches (66 cm) long

Materials

.012-inch beading wire

24 turquoise round beads, 6 mm

36 frosted amethyst E beads, size 6

26 frosted red E beads, size 6

17 olive bicone faceted beads, 6 mm

17 magenta round glass beads, 6 mm

6 amber tubular beads, 20 mm

170 amber seed beads

16 gold seed beads

1 gold spring ring clasp

6 gold crimp beads

15-inch (38.1 cm) length of 24-gauge gold wire

43 gold eyepins, 1½ inches (3.8 cm)

2 gold 3-hole connectors

55 gold jump rings, 3 mm

Tools

Needle-nose pliers

Round-nose pliers

Nylon-jaw pliers

Wire cutters

fig. 1   Eye pin assembly with one loop and beads

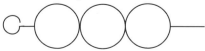

fig. 2   Eye pin assembly complete

Instructions

Load Eye Pins

1. Load 35 eye pins with ¾ inch (1.9 cm) of assorted beads. First form a loop on the end of the eyepin, then add the beads (figure 1). Make a loop on the other end with the round-nose pliers. The finished length should be ⅞ inch (2.2 cm) from loop to loop (figure 2). Wrap five of them with 3 inches (7.6 cm) of gold wire.

Make Wire Zig-Zags

2. Make eight wire zig-zags by holding the eye of an eye pin with the round-nose pliers. Use the tip of the needle-nose pliers to bend the stem of the eye pin back and forth into a zig-zag.

3. Form a loop at the opposite end with the round-nose pliers.

4. Flatten the zig-zag with the nylon-jaw pliers.

Assemble the Strands

5. Center strand: Attach 13 eye pins end to end with jump rings.

6. Middle strand: Attach 14 eye pins end to end with jump rings.

7. Outer strand: Attach 16 eye pins end to end with jump rings.

8. Attach the ends of each strand to a 3-hole connector with jump rings.

Assemble the Ends

9. Cut two 14-inch (35.6 cm) lengths of beading wire. Slide one half of the spring ring clasp to the center of one 14-inch length of stringing wire. Thread a crimp bead on the wires next to clasp. Crimp the bead.

10. Holding both wires together, thread:
    - 1 gold seed bead
    - 1 frosted red E bead
    - 1 gold seed bead
    - 17 amber seed beads
    - 1 gold seed bead
    - 3 frosted amethyst E beads
    - 1 gold seed bead
    - 17 amber seed beads
    - 1 gold seed bead
    - 1 magenta 6-mm bead
    - 1 gold seed bead
    - 17 amber seed beads
    - 1 gold seed bead
    - 1 olive 6-mm faceted bead
    - 1 gold seed bead

    (This will be about 4¼ inchs (10.8 cm) of beads.)

11. Separate the wires. Thread each wire with 17 amber seed beads and a crimp bead. Fold each wire over the outer holes of the 3-hole connector, then back through the crimp bead. Tighten the wire and crimp the bead. Thread the wire tails back through several amber seed beads. Cut the wire tails.

12. Repeat for the other side of the necklace, using the other half of the clasp.

queen victoria

This cameo necklace will add a touch of class to your jewelry collection.

Designers: Marty Stevens-Heebner & Christine Calla

Finished size: 12 inches (30.5 cm) long

Materials

Cameo, 40 x 30 mm

Bezel to hold the cameo

18-inch (45.7 cm) length of 24-gauge wire

7 rectangular carnelian beads, 15 x 10 mm

144 freshwater pearls, 4 mm

Clasp

3-inch (7.6 cm) length of chain

Head pin

Tools

Nylon-jaw pliers

Round-nose pliers

Wire cutters

Designer's Tip

For centuries cameos were obtainable only by the well-to-do, but the Industrial Revolution changed that. By the mid-1800s, cameos made in English factories from glass or Wedgwood porcelain paste were widely available and very popular. Now it seems that each new generation of jewelry lovers is drawn to this emblem of the Victorian era. Fetch that cameo from your mother's jewelry box, and claim it as your own!

Instructions

1. Lay the cameo inside the bezel and secure it by gently squeezing the top loop of the bezel with the nylon-jaw pliers. (Needle-nose pliers can also be used if the serrated edges are covered with masking tape to protect the bezel.)

2. Cut a 2½-inch (6.4 cm) piece of the 24-gauge wire. Grasp the wire ½ inch from the end with the round-nose pliers, make a loop by wrapping the wire around one of the prongs of the pliers, then slip it through the loop at the top of the bezel. Wrap the remaining wire two to three times around the base of the loop, and trim any excess. Slide a carnelian bead onto the wire, and make a loop in the opposite end approximately 8 mm in diameter. Wrap the wire two to three times between the loop and the bead, and trim any excess wire. Repeat this step to attach a second carnelian to the cameo.

3. Cut a 3½-inch (8.9 cm) piece of the 24-gauge wire, make a loop in one end with the pliers, and slip it through the large loop of one of the beaded wires from step 2. Wrap the wire as in step 2, then thread 12 freshwater pearls onto the wire. Repeat this step two more times so that you have a total of three wires with pearls attached.

4. Repeat step 2, this time hooking the first loop through the remaining end loops of the beaded wires from step 3. Then repeat step 3.

5. Repeat steps 3 and 4 on the other side of the necklace. Then repeat step 2 to attach an additional beaded wire to one end of the necklace, this time slipping the bottom of the clasp onto the second loop of the beaded wire.

6. Repeat step 2, this time slipping one of the end links of the piece of chain onto the second loop before wrapping it closed.

7. Slip a carnelian bead onto the headpin, make a loop in the end with the pliers, and thread it through the remaining end link of the chain. Wrap the wire two to three times between the loop and the bead, and trim any excess wire.

silver dragon

The most crucial step in this project comes at the start: finding a silver pendant and two large beads with just the right detail and patina to give this necklace the look of a treasured antique.

Materials

Designer: Andrea L. Stern

Finished size: 21 inches (53.3 cm) long

3 turquoise cones, 25 x 9 mm

3 silver head pins, each 3 inches
(7.6 cm) long

Chinese silver dragon pendant with
two loops on top and three loops on
bottom, 60 x 65 mm

4 12-inch (30.5 cm) pieces of 0.019-
inch (0.5 mm) flexible beading wire

6 crimp beads

16 Chinese turquoise beads, 4 mm

16 Chinese turquoise beads, ranging
from 6 to 7 mm

26 silver flower filler beads, 6 mm

28 Chinese turquoise beads, ranging
from 9 to 10 mm

2 Chinese silver dragon tubes,
50 x 15 mm

Hook-and-eye clasp

Tools

Chain-nose pliers

Ruler or tape measure

Wire cutters

Round-nose pliers

Scissors

Crimping pliers

Instructions

1. Use the turquoise cones to make three dangles by stringing each one onto a head pin. Use the chain-nose pliers to bend the wire 90° at the top, and then use the wire cutters to trim ⅝ inch (1.6 cm) from the end. After using the round-nose pliers to make a big loop, string each cone onto the bottom of the pendant and close the loop.

2. Measure and cut a 12-inch (30.5 cm) piece of the beading wire with the scissors. Slide the wire through a crimp bead, through the loop on one side of the dragon pendant, and then back through the crimp bead. Crimp with the crimping pliers. Trim the excess wire close to the bead. Repeat, sliding the second piece of wire through the same loop on the top of the pendant.

3. String beads onto each wire in the following order:
   • 4-mm Chinese turquoise bead
   • 6- to 7-mm Chinese turquoise bead
   • Silver flower bead
   • 9- to 10-mm Chinese turquoise bead
   • Silver flower bead
   • 6- to 7-mm Chinese turquoise bead
   • 4-mm Chinese turquoise bead

4. Slide both wires through the long silver dragon tube. (Hint: it's easier to slide one wire at a time.) Separate the wires and then repeat step 3.

5. After stringing both wires through a silver flower bead, string them through a 9- to 10-mm Chinese turquoise bead and a flower bead a total of four times.

6. String six more 9- to 10-mm Chinese turquoise beads onto both wires.

7. Pass both wires through a crimp bead, through one side of the clasp, and then back through the crimp bead and crimp. Trim close to the bead.

8. Repeat steps 2 through 7 on the other side of the pendant.

pearlescent

Luscious freshwater pearls are combined with the hard-edged
perfection of crystals to create this stunning necklace.

Designer: Christine Strube

Finished size: 22 inches (55.9 cm) long

Materials

28 pale green stick freshwater pearl beads, 6 x 17 mm

7 pale green round freshwater pearl beads, 6 to 7 mm

10 light green crystal round pearl beads, 6 mm

10 olive AB crystal round beads, 6 mm

7 dark amethyst AB crystal round beads, 6 mm

7 light amethyst AB crystal round beads, 6 mm

5 silver AB crystal cube beads, 6 mm

12 amethyst bicone beads, 4 mm

16 olive bicone beads, 4 mm

Purple iris seed beads, size 8°

Opaque green seed beads, size 11°

Purple iris seed beads, size 11°

12 light matte-green pressed-glass flower cap beads, 7 mm

7 amethyst pressed-glass flower beads, 8 mm

5 amethyst pressed-glass flower beads, 14 mm

5 matte-olive round beads, 8 mm

42 sterling silver 24-gauge head pins, 2 inches (5.1 cm)

2 gold-filled crimp beads, 2 x 2 mm

Gold box clasp set with peridot inset, 14 mm

22-inch (55.9 cm) length of gold .019 flexible beading wire

Tools

Chain-nose pliers

Round-nose pliers

Crimping pliers

Wire cutters

Instructions

1. Use one head pin to stack an arrangement of beads as outlined below. Secure the beads with a wrapped loop. You will make 30 bead dangles in all.

    Dangle A: String one crystal pearl bead and three purple size 11° seed beads. (Make six.)

   Dangle B: String one olive 4-mm crystal bicone bead, one green size 11° seed bead, and one small amethyst flower bead. (Make six.)

   Dangle C: String one amethyst 4-mm crystal bicone bead, one matte-green flower bead, and three purple size 11° seed beads. (Make ten.)

   Dangle D: String one purple size 11° seed bead, one purple size 8° seed bead, one olive 8-mm round bead, and one purple size 11° seed bead. (Make five.)

   Dangle E: String one purple size 11° seed bead and one pale green 7-mm freshwater pearl bead. (Make five).

   Dangle F: String one dark amethyst 6-mm crystal round bead and three green size 11° seed beads. (Make five.)

   Dangle G: String one olive 6-mm crystal round bead, two green size 11° seed beads, and one large amethyst flower bead. (Make five.)

2. Use the beading wire to string one crimp bead, one crystal pearl bead, and half of the clasp. Pass back through the crystal pearl bead and the crimp bead, leaving a 1-inch (2.5 cm) tail. Snug the beads and crimp the crimp bead. Cut the tail wire close to the crimp.

3. String one amethyst 4-mm bicone bead, one green flower bead from inside to outside, one small amethyst flower bead from inside to outside, one crystal pearl bead, one light amethyst 6-mm bead, one stick pearl bead, one round pearl bead, one purple size 11° seed bead, two stick pearl beads, and one dark amethyst 6-mm bead.

4. String one stick pearl bead, one dangle A, one dangle B, one stick pearl bead, one olive 4-mm bicone bead, one dangle C, one dangle D, one light amethyst 6-mm bead, one stick pearl bead, one dangle E, one dangle F, one stick pearl bead, one olive 4-mm bicone bead, one dangle G, one dangle C, and one cube. Repeat the sequence four more times to make five repetitions in all.

5. String one stick pearl bead, one dangle A, and one dangle B.

6. Repeat step 3 in reverse to string the other side of the necklace.

7. String one crimp bead, one crystal pearl bead, and the other half of the clasp. Pass back through the crystal pearl bead and the crimp bead.

Before crimping, hold the necklace up by the unfinished end. Use your fingers to adjust the beads so they sit nicely together, with little or no gaps between each. To make sure the beads are settled, but not strung too tightly, let the piece coil gently into your hands. If this movement isn't fluid, loosen the spacing a bit to reduce the tension on the beading wire. This will not only help with drape and comfort while you're wearing it, but will also help avoid wire abrasion and breakage.

8. Crimp the crimp bead. Trim any excess wire close to the crimp.

orbital

Tiny beads wrapped into these baubles add a dash of color.

Designer: Kathy Frey

Finished size: 19 inches (48.3 cm) long

Materials

45-foot (13.7 m) length of 22-gauge half-hard sterling silver wire

Hook-and-eye clasp

320 glass seed beads in various colors and finishes, size 11°

Tools

Round-nose pliers

Chain-nose pliers

Wire cutters

Planishing hammer

Steel block

Instructions

Lay out the balls so they are graduated from small (at the clasp ends) to large toward the center, arranging the bead colors randomly. Then fill in any size or color gaps by making specific balls for specific locations in the necklace. Make some extra-small balls for the very ends of the necklace and extra-large balls for the center, so the size transition is smooth and noticeable, and the necklace reaches 16 to 17 inches (40.6 to 43.2 cm) in length.

1. Use chain- and round-nose pliers to form a simple loop on one end of the wire. Approximately ¼ inch (6 mm) down from the loop, fold the wire loosely back on itself (don't flatten the wire together) to establish a central stem (photo 1). **Note:** The length of the stem determines the size of the ball; ¼ inch (6 mm) is on the small side, so vary the length of the stem for different ball sizes.

2. At the midpoint of the stem, use chain-nose pliers to bend the wrapping wire at a 90° angle. Wrap a loose, open spiral around the stem, working up toward the loop. It works best to hold the pliers parallel to the center post and use your fingers to wrap the wire around them (photo 2).

3. Start bending and working the wrapping wire around this central stem to form an open, airy sphere. As the ball gets bigger, make sure the wrapping wire starts touching the interior wires, creating a more solid and stable ball overall (photo 3).

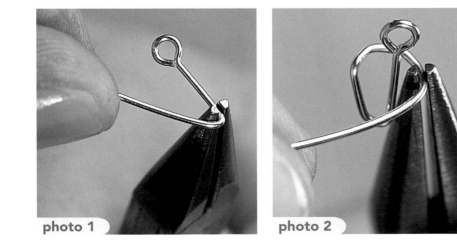

photo 1   photo 2

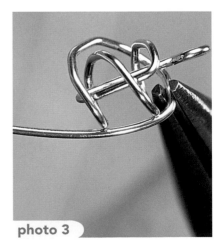

photo 3

4. When the sphere is roughly blocked out, start threading beads onto the wire and position them around the ball as you wrap (photo 4).

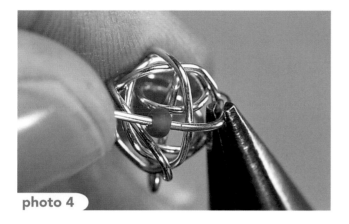

photo 4

5. When the ball is the desired size, pass the wire through its center, starting at the loop end and continuing through to the other side. Pull gently until the wire is taut (photo 5).

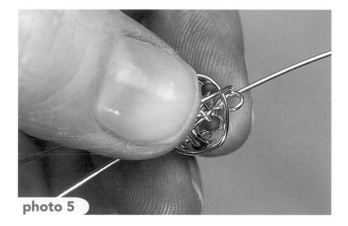

photo 5

6. Use chain-nose pliers to bend the tail at a 90° angle flat against the ball. Use wire cutters to flush cut the wire to loop length and use round-nose pliers to form a simple loop (photo 6). Try to make the loops perpendicular to each other. ***Note:*** If the starting loop gets slightly buried, grasp it flat with chain-nose pliers and pull it gently so it sticks out slightly.

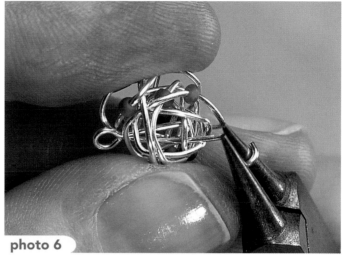

photo 6

7. Repeat steps 1 through 6 to make an assortment of 32 balls for a 17-inch (43.2 cm) necklace. Make balls in a variety of colors, creating two or three balls for each color bead or finish. Also, make sure to create differently sized balls, with 1- to 1½- feet (30.5 to 45.7 cm) long pieces of wire.

8. To assemble the necklace, lay out the balls in a graduated pattern from small to large, so that that the smaller balls are at the clasp ends and the larger balls are toward the center. ***Note:*** Make sure to arrange the bead colors randomly.

9. Link the balls together by connecting the simple loops at the sides of each ball. To connect the loops, first use flat-nose pliers to open a loop on one ball, just as you would a jump ring, then attach the next ball and close the loop.

10. Look for any size or color problems in the necklace. Maybe the ball size gradient is awkward at a point or a color is needed in one area. Make specific balls for these spots until the necklace is the desired length and hangs well.

11. Attach the hook-and-eye clasp.

turquoise spikes

This necklace is delicate yet edgy, interesting, and fun. The colors will brighten basic black, but the design would also pair well with a sundress and sandals.

Designer: Nancy Kugel

Finished length: 20 inches (50.8 cm) long

Materials

13 green turquoise spikes in graduated lengths

12 silver head pins, extra-long

24 garnet rounds, 3 mm

48 turquoise rounds, 8 mm

6 faceted garnet rounds, 4 mm

14 silver Bali heishi spacers

24 garnet seed beads

2 crimp tubes

Silver toggle clasp

20-inch (50.8 cm) length of flexible beading wire

Tools

Wire cutters

Round-nose pliers

Instructions

1. Lay out the spikes in the order you prefer. You may want to string them in a random pattern, as shown, or may prefer a more graduated look.

2. Next, string each head pin with a seed bead, an 8-mm turquoise round, and another 3-mm garnet. If you're making a necklace with a random pattern, use the wire cutters to trim the head pins to different lengths. For a graduated pattern, trim each head pin to be slightly shorter than the spike next to it. Use the round-nose pliers to make a small wrapped loop at the top of each head pin.

3. On a length of flexible beading wire, string a spike, then a 3-mm garnet, a head pin with beads, and a 3-mm garnet. Repeat this sequence until you finish with your last spike. Center this grouping of beads on the beading wire.

4. On one side, string an 8-mm turquoise round. Then string a spacer, a 4-mm faceted garnet, a spacer, and five 8-mm turquoise rounds, repeating this sequence until you reach the desired length. Repeat this pattern on the other side.

5. To finish, string three 3-mm garnets and a crimp tube on the end. Loop the wire through the ring on one side of the toggle clasp, then take the wire back through the crimp and several beads. Use the crimping pliers to crush the crimp. Trim any excess wire. Repeat on the other side.

odyssey

This designer used bold glass beads and branching links to create an unusual geometric piece with lean, high-tech style. Despite looking complex, the necklace is actually quite simple to make.

Instructions

1. You will make three different strands. For the first strand, place the following, in order, on an eye pin: a second eye pin, followed by a black pyramid bead, a silver tube bead, and a crimp bead. Hammer the end of the first eye pin to flatten it, then file the rough ends.

2. On the second eye pin, slip a third eye pin, followed by three gray tube beads, a silver tube bead, and a crimp bead. As before, flatten and file the end of the second eye pin.

3. On the third eye pin, repeat what you did with the first eye pin. With the fourth eye pin, repeat what you did with the second eye pin. Keep alternating bead patterns until you've used 19 eye pins. Don't add an eye pin to the 19th eye pin, only a black pyramid bead, a silver tube bead, and a crimp bead. Finish the end of the last eye pin with a loop.

4. For the second strand, work in the same manner as the first strand, but with a different bead pattern. On the first eye pin, add a second eye pin, then three gray tube beads, a silver tube bead, and a crimp bead. Hammer and file as before. On the second eye pin, add the third eye pin, a white glass bead, a silver tube bead, and a crimp bead. Hammer and file the end. On the third eye pin, repeat what you added to the first eye pin in this strand. On the

fourth, add a red glass bead, a silver tube bead, and a crimp. Again, hammer and file. The fifth eye pin has the same beads as the first eye pin. For the sixth one, add a black glass bead, a silver tube bead, and a crimp. Hammer and file as before. Repeat the pattern, alternating white, red, and black glass beads on the even-numbered eye pins, until you have strung 19 eye pins together. As in the first strand, the 19th eye pin has no eye pin added onto it; instead, add only three gray tube beads, a silver tube bead, and a crimp bead. Finish the end of the 19th eye pin with a loop.

5. The third strand differs from the others only in its bead pattern. On the first eye pin and all subsequent odd-numbered ones, add a second eye pin, then a black pyramid bead, a silver tube bead, and a crimp bead. Hammer and file the first eye pin. As in the second strand, the even-numbered eye pins get an additional eye pin, a glass bead, a silver tube bead, and a crimp bead added to them, but the color pattern changes to red, then black, then white, and repeats as before, until you have strung 19 eye pins together. As in the first strand, the 19th eye pin gets no eye pin added onto it, only a black pyramid bead, a silver tube bead, and a crimp bead. As before, the end of the 19th eye pin is finished with a loop.

6. Open the first and last loops on all three strands. Attach all the first loops to one jump ring, and all the last loops to another. Attach one half of the clasp to each jump ring.

Designer: Ellen Gerritse

Finished size: 16 inches (40.6 cm) long

Materials

20 black pyramid-style stone beads, 6 mm

57 sterling silver tube beads, 6 mm

57 sterling silver crimp beads, 1.3 mm

57 matte-gray Japanese tube beads, 3 mm

6 assorted white glass beads, 15 mm

6 assorted red glass beads, 15 mm

6 assorted black glass beads, 15 mm

57 sterling silver eye pins, 1½ inches (3.8 cm)

2 medium sterling silver jump rings

1 sterling silver clasp and hook

Tools

Hammer and block

spotlight

A large blue topaz is the focal point for this stunning necklace, with seed beads adding artistic detail.

Designer: Valérie MacCarthy

Finished size: 16¼ inches (41.3 cm); focal element, 2⅞ inches (7.3 cm)

Materials

1 large blue topaz, 40 mm

6 blue topaz briolettes, 10 mm

5 light blue chalcedony briolettes, 10 mm

4 blue topaz beads, 3 mm

1 gold-filled bead, 3 mm

Brown seed beads

6 to 8 gold-filled ball-end head pins, 1½ inches (3.8 cm) long

1 gold-filled ball-end head pin, 2 inches (5.1 cm)

1 gold-filled hook-and-eye clasp

15-inch (38.1 cm) length of gold-filled krinkle chain, 4 mm

24-inch (61 cm) length of 24-gauge gold-filled wire

8-inch (20.3 cm) length of 22-gauge gold-filled wire

Tools

Chain-nose pliers

Round-nose pliers

Wire cutters

Large rubberized round-nose pliers

Ruler

Instructions

1. Cut the gold-filled krinkle chain into three 1-inch (2.5 cm) segments and one 12-inch (30.5 cm) segment. Before cutting short chain segments, always count the links to make certain that the segments are exactly the same length.

2. Using the round-nose pliers, make a loop in the 24-gauge wire about ¾ inch (1.9 cm) from the end. Take one of the 1-inch (2.5 cm) chain segments and place an end link onto the loop. Hold the loop with the chain-nose pliers and twist the wires together. Cut off the shorter wire end.

3. Holding the loop with the chain-nose pliers, bend the wire about 45°. Make a new loop with the round-nose pliers.

fig. 1

4. Select the 12-inch (30.5 cm) chain segment and fold it in half to locate the center link in the chain. Attach the loop made in step 3 to this center link. Hold the loop with the chain-nose pliers and wrap the wire around the twist you made in step 2 (figure 1). Cut off the excess wire.

5. Select the 2-inch (5.1 cm) head pin and slide the 3-mm gold-filled bead onto it, followed by the large 40-mm topaz. Bend the wire of the head pin 45°, and wrap it around the round-nose pliers.

6. Attach the head pin loop to the end of the 1-inch (2.5 cm) chain. Hold the loop with the chain-nose pliers and wrap the wire to secure. Cut off the excess wire.

7. Select ten 10-mm briolettes (five each of blue topaz and light blue chalcedony) and attach them along the 1-inch (2.5 cm) chain with the 24-gauge wire. Use the following method: Slide ¾ inch (1.9 cm) of the wire through each briolette and bend up both wire ends until they cross. Twist the wires together to secure. Cut off the shorter wire end. Bend the longer wire 45°, and wrap it around the round-nose pliers. Slide the wire through one of the links in the 1-inch (2.5. cm) chain. Hold the loop with the chain-nose pliers and wrap the wire around the first twist in the wire. Evenly space the 10 briolettes throughout the 1-inch (2.5. cm) chain.

8. Twirl six to eight head pins using the following technique. Wrap the pin around one jaw of the round-nose pliers by taking hold of the ball-end of the pin and twirling it around (figure 2). To continue the twist, release the pliers, rotate the pin slightly, grab on with the pliers again, and twist. Because the pliers are tapered, you'll need to be careful not to taper your twist. So to keep it even, flip the head pin when it is halfway done and continue wrapping it around the jaw. Leave a straight length of ¾ inch (1.9 cm) at the end (figure 3).

fig. 2   fig. 3

9. Select the brown seed beads and slide them onto a twirled head pin, stopping when you reach the straight part of the pin. Repeat for all of the head pins.

10. Attach the bead-covered head pins to the 1-inch (2.5 cm) section of chain, intermixing the head pins among the briolettes. Using the round-nose pliers, hold the straight end of each head pin and wrap it around to form a loop. Attach this loop to one of the chain links between two briolettes. Hold the loop with the chain-nose pliers and wrap the wire around to secure. Cut off the excess wire. Repeat this step to attach all of the head pins, forming a cluster around the large topaz.

11. Begin working on the closure of the necklace. To add interest and detail, you'll be removing some of the chain length and replacing it with beaded wire in the steps that follow.

12. Using the round-nose pliers, make a loop in the 22-gauge wire by holding the wire about ¾ inch (1.9 cm) from the end and wrapping it around. Attach this loop to one of the 12-inch (30.5 cm) chain ends. Hold the loop with the chain-nose pliers and twist to secure. Cut off the shorter wire end.

13. Slide 1½ inches (3.8 cm) of seed beads and two 3-mm topaz beads onto the wire. Bend the wire 45°, and again wrap it around the round-nose pliers. Slide a clasp onto this loop, then hold the loop with the chain-nose pliers and wrap the wire around to secure. Cut off the excess wire.

14. Bend the beaded wire ever so slightly to conform to the curve of the neck.

15. Repeat steps 12 through 14 on the other end of the 12-inch (30.5 cm) chain, this time placing a 1-inch (2.5 cm) length of chain onto the loop in step 13, instead of a clasp.

16. If you choose, you can make a clasp from wire instead of using a purchased one. To make a clasp, begin with the 22-gauge wire and the round-nose pliers, making a loop in the wire about ¾ inch (1.9 cm) from the end. Attach the loop to the end of the 1½-inch (3.8 cm) beaded wire end. Hold this loop with the chain-nose pliers and wrap the wire around to secure. Cut off the excess wire.

17. With the rubberized round-nose pliers, wrap around the wire to form a loop. Put the round-nose pliers around the wire at the same level as the wrapped wire section, and then loop the wire around (figure 4). Cut off the excess wire.

fig. 4

18. Make the catch by forming a new loop in the 22-gauge wire. Slide this loop through the wire loop at the end of the beaded wire. Twist the wires together to secure. Cut off the shorter wire end.

19. Grip the wire with the rubberized round-nose pliers and wrap the wire around. Hold the loop with these same pliers and wrap the wire around the twist you made in step 18 to secure. Cut off the excess wire.

20. For a final detail on the toggle chain, make a loop in the 22-gauge wire using the round-nose pliers. Slide the wire through the smaller loop of the catch to attach the loops to each other. Hold this loop with the chain-nose pliers and twist the wires around to secure. Cut off the shorter wire end.

21. Make a new loop using the round-nose pliers and place the remaining 1-inch (2.5 cm) length of chain onto this loop. Grip the loop with the chain-nose pliers and wrap the wire around the twist you made in step 20 to secure. Cut off the excess wire.

22. Slide the 24-gauge wire through the one remaining blue topaz 10-mm briolette so that ¾ inch (1.9 cm) extends from one end. Bend both ends upward until they cross. Twist the wires together and cut off the shorter wire end.

23. Make a loop with the round-nose pliers and string it through the end of the chain. Hold the loop with the chain-nose pliers and wrap the wire around the twisted part to secure. Cut off the excess wire. This chain section can play the part of a back detail as well as a toggle to extend the length of the necklace.

flight
of fancy

Random bead placement on multiple strands
of memory wire lets this piece evolve in unexpected ways.

Designer: Ndidi Kowalczyk

Finished size: 13 inches (33 cm) long

Materials

20 to 50 fire-polished beads, pearls, or semiprecious stones, 3 to 8 mm

1 brass focal bead, 20 mm

3 to 4 strands fire-polished faceted beads, 6 mm

1 to 2 strands, each at least 16 inches (40.6 cm) long, of garnet-color tumbled stone chips, 3 to 4 mm

6 dove beads (center drilled), 8 mm

4 crystals, 4 mm

1 strand of filed brass cube beads, 3 mm

Vitrail oval crystal, 24 mm

3 to 4 strands potato pearls, 8 mm

1 antique brass finish bezel cup with loop, 20 mm

Locket, 45 mm

6 lockets, 20 to 25 mm

6 small charms, slightly smaller than each locket (except largest locket)

2 biplane charms, 18 mm

2 brass bead caps to fit the brass focal bead

7 head pins, 2 inches (5 cm) long

14 antique brass finish jump rings, 5 mm

2 split rings, 5 mm

Antique brass finish lobster clasp

2 antique brass finish 10-loop end bars

2 cone ends, 6 mm

(continued on next page)

Instructions

1. Use the all-in-one glue to attach and seal decorative and blue paper to the back and interior of the bezel cup and some of the lockets.

2. Place—do not glue—a charm inside the bezel cup and each locket except the largest one. Close the lockets to make sure they will snap shut with the object inside.

3. Lightly coat the interior bezel cup and lockets with the all-in-one glue to attach the charms and embellish them with fire polish beads, pearls, or semiprecious stones. Pour the clear craft lacquer inside each locket.

4. Make a link using the bead caps and the large brass focal bead. Before closing the wrapped loop at the bottom, add a short length of the base metal cable chain. Close the top with a simple loop. Attach the large locket to the bottom of the chain. Create two small dangles to attach along the chain.

5. Make a wrapped loop at the end of a head pin. Cut the head off the head pin. Thread a dove bead and a 4-mm crystal onto the head pin. Make another wrapped loop. Make two more links like this. Use a jump ring to add a locket to the bottom of a dove link. Attach a charm to each of the remaining dove links.

6. Make a wrapped loop dangle on a head pin threaded with a brass cube bead and fire-polished bead. Attach this to another link that has only a dove bead.

7. Without cutting off the head on a head pin, make a dangle with a small crystal and dove bead. Using a jump ring, attach two links from the base metal chain to the top of the dove bead.

8. Using jump rings, create three dangles by attaching a locket to a ¾-inch (1.9 cm) piece of base metal chain. Make and set aside the following dangles, for use in step 14: Thread a cube and dove bead onto a head pin, and use a simple loop to attach it to the chain on one of the locket dangles. Add a large bead (threaded on a head pin) to another locket dangle. Use a jump ring to add a biplane charm to another locket dangle.

Materials (continued)

Stainless steel memory wire necklace with large loops

20-inch (50.8 cm) length of base metal cable chain, 4 mm

4-inch (10.2 cm) length of base metal cable chain, 4 mm

5-inch (12.7 cm) square of decorative paper

6-inch (15.2 cm) square of blue paper

Water-based, clear-drying all-in-one glue, sealant, and finish

Clear craft lacquer

Tools

2 pairs of chain-nose pliers

Round-nose pliers

Flush wire cutters

Memory wire shears

Small paintbrush

Small tweezers

Split-ring pliers

9. Cut a ⅜-inch (1 cm) piece of base metal chain. Attach the vitrail oval crystal to one end, using a jump ring.

10. Cut five lengths of memory wire, each with one full rotation plus 3 inches (7.6 cm). Cut three lengths of chain, each 2 inches (5 cm) long, for the spacer bars. Slide an end-link of a spacer bar chain to the center of a length of memory wire.

Designer's Tip

The loops in at least 11 inches (27.9 cm) of the base metal chain must be large enough for the memory wire to feed through. The remaining chain lengths, which are used to join the memory wire loops, can be scrap chain.

11. Add any combination of pearl, cube, stone chip, and fire-polished beads to the memory wire, on both sides of the spacer bar chain, ending with a pearl. Continue to string any combination of items until you have covered 1 inch (2.5 cm) of wire on one side of the chain and ¾ inch (1.9 cm) on the other. Slide the top link of the vitrail crystal dangle onto one side and the dove bead dangle on the other.

12. Cover 2 inches (5.1 cm) on both sides of the chain. Add the next length of spacer bar chain (figure 1). Continue filling the memory wire, for 1 inch (2.5 cm) on both sides.

fig. 1

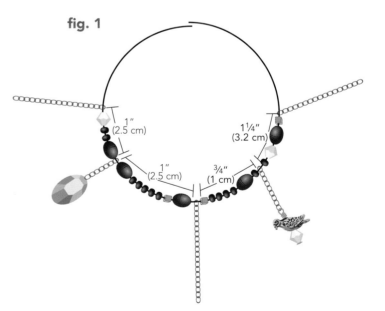

13. Thread another length of the cut memory wire onto the center spacer bar chain, ¼ inch (6 mm) below the link holding the first length of memory wire. String items to cover 2 inches (5 cm) on both sides of the wire (figure 2). Insert the wire through the next length of spacer bar chain. Continue filling the memory wire, randomly adding the dangles you made earlier. Add and cover two more lengths of memory wire in the same manner.

fig. 2

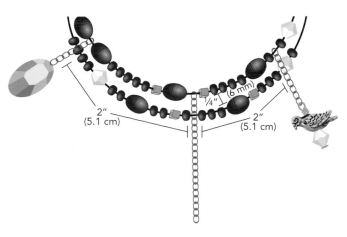

2"
(5.1 cm)

¼" (6 mm)

2"
(5.1 cm)

14. Add the last length of memory wire to the central spacer bar chain. String 1 inch (2.5 cm) of pearls and beads to the wire, on each side of the spacer chain. On each side, string one of the dangles that you set aside in step 8. Secure these with several beads and then a pearl. Continue filling the memory wire, randomly adding dangles until just ½ inch (1.3 cm) of the wire remains exposed at the ends.

15. Use the split rings to attach the lobster clasp parts to the end bars, adding a biplane charm to one side. Attach the end bars to the necklace, using the round-nose pliers to turn simple loops in the memory wire and connect these to the spacer bar loops. Use the pair of chain-nose pliers to push down on the memory wire loops to close them. Use a 5-mm jump ring to connect a charm or dangle to the last ring of both end bars.

16. Attach the extender chain to one of the split rings. Add a dangle at the bottom of the extender, using a teardrop crystal, head pin, and cone.

baltic elegance

Some people believe amber can help improve your luck, strength, and love life.
Wear this necklace to transform negative energy to positive.

Designer: Patty Cox

Finished size: 15 inches (38.1 cm) long

Materials

26 Baltic amber oval beads

Mahogany seed beads, 8 x 12 mm

19 bronze faceted Czech glass beads, 4 mm

14 bronze faceted Czech glass beads, 6 mm

24 fluted 24-kt. gold-plated beads, 4 mm

12 fluted 24-kt. gold-plated beads, 5 mm

22 fluted 24-kt. gold-plated beads, 6 mm

1 gold-filled filigree clasp

2 gold head pins

2 gold crimp beads

Beading wire, .015

Tools

Wire cutters

Crimping tool

Round-nose pliers

Ruler

fig. 1

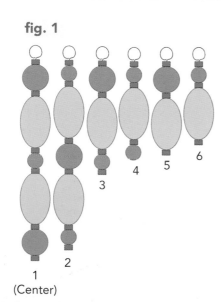

1
(Center)

2

3

4

5

6

Instructions

1. To make the head pin dangles, thread the beads on the head pins according to figure 1, making 23 beaded head pin dangles in all.

2. Cut each head pin wire ⅜ inch (1 cm) from the last bead. Form a loop in the wire end using round-nose pliers.

3. Cut a 24-inch (61 cm) length of beading wire. Thread a crimp bead on the wire end. Thread the wire end through one side of the clasp, then back through the crimp bead, leaving a 1-inch (2.5 cm) tail. Crimp the bead.

4. To make one side of the necklace, begin with a seed bead, twelve 4-mm gold beads, and six 5-mm gold beads. Add a seed bead between each of the gold beads. Thread the first beads on the wire and over the wire tail.

5. To make the front part of the necklace, add a seed bead, a head pin side dangle, and a 6-mm gold bead. Continue adding seed beads, head pin dangles, and 6-mm gold beads to complete the front of the necklace. See the legend below regarding the placement of the dangles.

6. Finish the other side of the necklace, adding six 5-mm gold beads, then twelve 4-mm gold beads with a seed bead between each gold bead.

7. Add a gold crimp bead on the end of the wire. Thread the wire end through the other side of the clasp, then back through the crimp bead and several beads. Pull the wire taut. Crimp the bead. Cut the wire tail.

The Beaded Dangles Legend

1. (Center) Make one. Sequence: Seed bead, 6-mm faceted, seed bead, amber, seed bead, 4-mm faceted, seed bead, amber, seed bead, 6-mm faceted, seed bead.

2. Make two and put one on each side of the center dangle. Sequence: Seed bead, 4-mm faceted, seed bead, amber, seed bead, 6-mm faceted, seed bead, amber, seed bead, 4-mm faceted, seed bead.

3. Make two and put one on each side of the center dangle. Sequence: Seed bead, 6-mm faceted, seed bead, amber, seed bead, 4-mm faceted, seed bead.

4. Make two and put one on each side of the center dangle. Sequence: Seed bead, 4-mm faceted, seed bead, amber, seed bead, 4-mm faceted.

5. Make eight and put four on each side of the center dangle. Sequence: Seed bead, 6-mm faceted, seed bead, amber, seed bead.

6. Make eight and put four on each side of the center dangle. Sequence: Seed bead, 4-mm faceted, seed bead, amber, seed bead.

* **Note:** Alternate dangles #5 and #6 when placing them in the sequence.

lace

This simple necklace
features a whitewashed filigree
rosette beaded with glass pearls.
The mix of whitewashed metal and
brass makes the design casual. The
double chain allows you to wear it
long or short.

Instructions

1. Cut the chain into two 18-inch (45.7 cm) sections with one oval link at each end. Set aside.

2. Heat-treat the rosettes and clean them so they're free of lint or dust. Set aside.

3. Working in a well-ventilated area, set a few sheets of newsprint or scrap cardboard down to protect your work surface. Spray the front of both rosettes with a thin coat of clear paint. Immediately spray a thin coat of white over the clear paint and use a cloth to rub the paint from the surface. Some paint will remain in the details of the filigree. To add or reduce the amount of paint in the finish, spray the rosettes with white paint again. Immediately wipe the paint. Once you are pleased with the effect, allow the paint to dry for two hours. After it has dried, apply two thin coats of clear paint, allowing the paint to dry thoroughly between coats. Set aside.

4. Repeat step 3 with the chain sections. Take care to thoroughly wipe the chain from end to end.

5. Slide one 8-mm bead and the bead cap, inside to outside, onto a head pin. Form a simple loop to secure the bead and cap. Set this long dangle aside.

6. Slip one 3-mm bead onto a head pin. Form a simple loop to secure the bead. Repeat to make small dangles with all the 3-mm beads. Set aside.

7. Attach one small dangle to each of the center oval links that sit between the chain's long tube sections (figure 1). There should be one remaining link. Set aside.

fig. 1

Designer: Cynthia Deis

Finished size: 36 inches (0.9 m) long

Materials

2 brass filigree rosettes, 30 mm

59 white glass pearl round beads, 3 mm

White glass pearl round bead, 8 mm

Antiqued brass petal bead cap, 6 mm

43 antiqued brass 22-gauge head pins, 1 inch (2.5 cm)

Antiqued brass 20-gauge head pin, 1 inch (2.5 cm)

Antiqued brass square jump ring, ¼ inch (6 mm)

3 antiqued brass round jump rings, 7 mm

Antiqued brass spring ring clasp, 15 mm

36-inch (91.4 cm) length of antiqued brass filled tube chain, 2 x 15 mm

12-inch (30.8 cm) length of medium-width flexible beading wire

Clear enamel spray paint

White enamel spray paint

Newsprint or scrap cardboard

Soft cloth

Tools

Wire cutters

Round-nose pliers

Chain-nose pliers

8. Place the rosettes back to back, edges aligned. Pass the beading wire through a hole at the edge of the two pieces and tie a square knot, leaving a 4-inch (10.2 cm) tail (figure 2).

String on one 3-mm bead and sew around the edge of the rosettes, passing through the next hole (figure 3). Repeat around to add sixteen 3-mm beads in all. Tie a square knot with the working and tail wires and trim close to the knot. Set the pendant aside.

9. Open a round jump ring and attach it to a hole at the edge of the pendant. Slip on the long dangle and close the ring. Attach a round jump ring to a hole on the opposite edge of the ring just placed (figure 4).

10. Use the square jump ring to connect one end of each chain length and the top of the pendant (figure 5).

11. Use chain-nose pliers to gently open the loop on the spring ring clasp. Attach the open ends of the chain and close the loop.

12. Open a round jump ring and slide on the remaining small dangle and the clasp loop. Close the ring (figure 6). To wear the necklace short, connect the clasp to the square jump ring. To wear it long, simply separate the chains and slip the necklace over your head.

fig. 2

fig. 3

fig. 4

fig. 5

fig. 6

bronze drops

A single Tahitian pearl, showcased in a handmade open spiral cap, hangs amid clusters of smaller pearls. The setting allows the pearls' natural shape, magnificent luster, and color variations to shine.

Designer: Sandra Lupo

Finished Size: 18 inches (45.7 cm) long

Materials

1 dark green Tahitian pearl, 10 x 14-mm teardrop, un-drilled or half-drilled

12 peridot button freshwater pearls, 4 mm

6 dark gray round freshwater pearls, 4 mm

12 light gray round freshwater pearls, 3 mm

12 semiprecious peridot faceted rondelles, 4 mm

24 gold-filled head pins, 1 inch (2.1 cm)

6 gold-filled 22-gauge oval jump rings, 4 x 5 mm

1 gold-filled toggle clasp, 6 mm

16-inch (40.6 cm) length of oval twist link gold-filled chain, or desired length, 4 mm

12-inch (30.5 cm) length of manufactured twist wire, or 2-foot (61 cm) length of 24-gauge, soft, gold-filled wire

Two-part 5-minute epoxy glue

(continued on next page)

Instructions

1. Slide two peridot pearls onto a head pin. Make a simple loop to secure the pearls. Repeat with all of the peridot pearls to make six bead dangles in all. Continue creating bead dangles in this fashion, making six using two light gray pearls each; six using two semiprecious peridot beads each; and six using one dark gray pearl each. Set the 24 bead dangles aside.

2. If you need to make your own twisted wire, fold the 24-gauge wire in half and place each of the wire ends into the chuck of the wire twister or pin vise. Stabilize the looped wire end by clamping it onto a table or other surface (figure 1). Turn the reel of the twister or pin vise in one direction until you are pleased with the level of twist. *Note:* The tighter you twist wire, the harder it will become, making it more difficult to work with later. You may want to experiment with a length of copper or brass wire first to find the optimum twist level. Remove the wire from the twister and clamp and trim each wire end. You should end up with about 10 inches (25.4 cm) of twisted wire.

    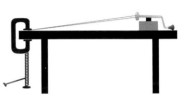

    fig. 1

3. Use the chain-nose pliers to make a ¼-inch (6 mm) right-angle bend at the end of the wire and form a three-coil wrapped loop at the bend. When you turn the loop, make it 3 to 4 mm in diameter. *Note:* There will be a short stem of wire below the wrapped loop. Don't trim it—you will use this to attach the large pearl.

4. Use the long end of the wire to form a spiral that fits over the top of the pearl, creating a wire bead cap (figure 2). Use the top of the pearl as your guide, but take care not to mar the pearl's nacre. Pull the spiral slightly apart so it forms to the pearl's shape.

    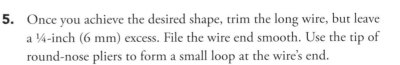

    fig. 2

5. Once you achieve the desired shape, trim the long wire, but leave a ¼-inch (6 mm) excess. File the wire end smooth. Use the tip of round-nose pliers to form a small loop at the wire's end.

Tools (continued)

Chain-nose pliers

Round-nose pliers

Flush cutters

Wire twister and clamp or pin vise (unnecessary if manufactured wire is used)

Needle file or emery board

Pearl holder

Fine-point permanent marker

Small drill and 1-mm chisel drill bit (if using an undrilled pearl)

6. If necessary, drill a small vertical hole at the top of the pearl. Place the pearl vertically, top side up, into the pearl holder to keep it stable. Mark the place where you want to drill. Drill into that mark until you reach one-third of the way down the pearl's center. *Note:* It may help to keep a small amount of cool water nearby to wet the drill bit, keeping it and the pearl cool during drilling. Let the pearl dry, blow out any excess dust, and set aside.

7. Use a small amount of epoxy to thoroughly coat the spiral cap's straight wire. Fit the wire into the pearl (figure 3). Use a cushioned support or clamp to hold the pearl and cap in place while the epoxy dries.

fig. 3

8. Use two jump rings to attach the pendant's loop to a link at the center of the chain.

9. Count four links down one side of the chain from the link to which you added the pendant. Add one of each type of bead dangle to this link. Count four more links down the chain and add another four bead dangles. Repeat one more time so you have three bead clusters in all. Repeat this step down the chain on the other side of the pendant.

10. Use two jump rings to attach one half of the clasp to one end of the chain. Repeat at the other end of the chain.

lucky

The carved charm on this spectacular necklace might attract good fortune. Though the bead links look ornate, they consist of just a few simple elements.

Designer: Mami Laher

Finished size: 27 inches (68.6 cm) long

Materials

25 assorted honey-colored glass beads, 5 mm

4 dichroic glass cube beads, 9 mm

12 faceted beads, 1 cm

4 rondelles, 1 cm

2 flat stone beads, 1 inch (2.5 cm)

Round carved charm, 1¾ inches (4.4 cm)

49-inch (1.2 m) length of 20-gauge gold-filled square wire for the caged bead links

48-inch (1.2 m) length of 22-gauge gold-filled square wire for the caged bead links

27-inch (68.6 cm) length of 18-gauge gold-filled wire for making bead loop links

4¼-inch (10.8 cm) length of 16-gauge gold-filled wire for the clasp and a connection element

28 jump rings, 18-gauge gold filled, 5 mm

2 jump rings, 18-gauge gold filled, 9 mm

1 jump ring, 18-gauge gold filled, 3 mm

Tools

Tape measure

Wire cutters

2 pairs of flat-nose pliers

2 pairs of round-nose pliers

Tabletop vise

Hammer and block

Instructions

1. Cut and twist four 8-inch (20.3 cm) pieces of 20-gauge square wire.

2. Cut two pieces of twisted wire, each 3½ inches (8.9 cm) long. Cut one 4¼-inch (10.8 cm) piece of untwisted 20-gauge square wire. Slip two 5-mm beads on each twisted wire and one glass cube on the untwisted wire and place them side by side (figure 1), shaping the wires into bundles at the ends.

3. Cut two 6-inch (15.2 cm) pieces of 22-gauge square wire. Clamp the end of one in the vise and wrap the other end four times around one of the bundled wire ends; repeat for the other end. Make spirals out of all six wire ends. Repeat the process to make a total of four caged-bead links.

4. Using the 18-gauge wire, make bead loop links out of each faceted bead, rondelle, stone bead, and the remaining 5-mm beads.

5. To make the clasp, use a 2¼-inch (5.7 cm) piece of 16-gauge wire. Shape it as shown in figure 2, then forge the large curves. Adjust the clasp's form if necessary.

6. To assemble one side of the chain, attach the links with 5-mm jump rings. For the caged bead links, pass the jump ring through the spiral of the center wire. The parts are assembled with faceted beads alternating with a caged bead, a stone, a caged bead, and ending with two rondelles and two 5-mm beads. On the end with a 5-mm bead, attach the clasp with a jump ring.

fig. 1

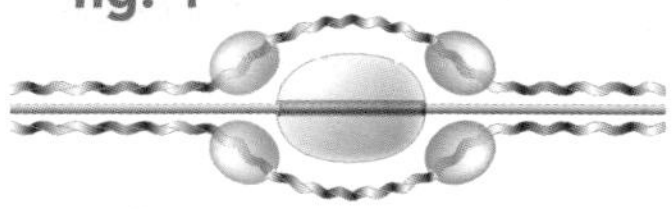

fig. 2

fig. 3

7. Make a second chain, as described in the previous step, but on the end with the 5-mm bead, use a 5-mm jump ring to attach a 9-mm jump ring.

8. An extra length of chain will be added to the 9-mm jump ring. To make it, link together the five remaining bead loops by their loops. Use the 3 mm jump ring to hang one end of the chain to the 5-mm jump ring.

9. Cut a 2-inch (5.1 cm) piece of 16-gauge wire and shape it like figure 3. Use the last 9-mm jump ring to hang the charm from the central loop of this element. Attach a chain through the center of each spiral with a 5-mm jump ring.

dangle

Display more than a dozen of your favorite large gemstones
with a necklace designed to enhance their translucent beauty.

Designer: Valérie MacCarthy

Finished size: 19½ inches (48.3 cm); longest
dangle, 4¾ inches (12 cm)

Materials

18 large watermelon tourmaline stones, 12 to 20 mm

9 peridot beads (oval), 8 mm

7 aventurine beads, 4 mm

10 pink tourmaline rondelles, 3 mm

6 chrysoprase rondelles, 8 mm

10 garnet beads, 4 mm

4 gold-filled beads, 2 mm

5 gold-filled beads, 3 mm

5 gold-filled ball-end head pins, 1½ inches
(3.8 cm) long

1 gold-filled lobster clasp

48-inch (122 cm) length of gold-filled chain, 1.5 mm

2-inch (5.1 cm) length of gold-filled chain (for the
toggle), 2.5 mm

60-inch (152.4 cm) length of 24-gauge
gold-filled wire

Tools

Chain-nose pliers

Round-nose pliers

Wire cutters

Large rubberized chain-nose pliers

Ruler

Instructions

1. This necklace is casual in its design, with the stones
    interspersed along the strands, connected by varying
    lengths of chain. The only technique you really need
    to know is how to make twisted wire bead links.
    Select and set aside the largest and/or most beautiful
    of the tourmaline stones to use in a focal position
    in step 9.

2. Using the round-nose pliers and the 24-gauge wire,
    make a loop in the wire about ¾ inch (1.9 cm) from
    the end. Slide this loop onto the chain. Hold the wire
    with the chain-nose pliers and twist the wires around
    to secure. Cut off the shorter wire end.

3. Slide one large tourmaline stone onto the wire. Bend
    the wire 45°. Hold the wire with the round-nose
    pliers and loop the wire around to secure.

4. Cut the chain you previously attached, making it
    between ½ to 2½ inches (1.3 to 5.1 cm) in length.

5. Place the remaining chain onto this loop. Hold the
    loop with the round-nose pliers and wrap the wire
    around to secure. Cut off the excess wire.

6. Make a new loop in the wire ¾ inch (1.9 cm) from
    the end. Run the loop onto the last link in the
    already-connected chain. Hold this loop and twist the
    wires around to secure. Cut off the shorter wire end.

7. Slide a variety of smaller beads onto the wire. For
    example: 4-mm round stone, 2-mm gold-filled bead,
    8-mm rondelle, 2-mm gold-filled bead, and 4-mm
    round stone. Another example: 3-mm rondelle,
    8-mm oval bead, and 3-mm rondelle. Feel free to mix
    and match the small stones in any order you wish in
    a fashion similar to the examples above, or in another
    design of your choosing. After you've added the
    beads, add a new length of chain to each twisted loop
    link and wrap the loop to secure.

8. Continue placing the large tourmaline stones and the smaller beads and stones on this length of chain until you've completed 8 inches (20.3 cm). Stretch out this completed strand in front of you and start working on the second 8-inch (20.3 cm) length. You'll need to complete a total of six 8-inch (20.3 cm) strands for the necklace. As you're working on the subsequent strands, be sure to periodically place them next to the completed ones to see how the stones are lining up in relation to each other. Avoid massing the stones in one area, and be sure to alternate the colors.

9. After the six strands are completed, you're ready to place the focal tourmaline stone that you set aside in step 1. Make a new wire loop with the 24-gauge wire. Place the end links of all six strands on this loop. Hold the loop with the round-nose pliers and twist the wires around to secure. Cut off the shorter wire end.

10. Slide the large tourmaline stone onto the wire. Bend the wire 45°. Hold it with the round-nose pliers and loop the wire around, but do not wrap it just yet (figure 1). Set it aside while you work on other parts of the necklace.

fig. 1

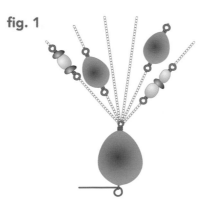

11. Repeat steps 2 through 7 to make four more lengths of chain, each about 1½ to 2½ inches (3.8 to 6.4 cm) in length, varying the length slightly for each piece of chain.

12. Finish off each piece of chain. First, place a variety of stones on one head pin. Then bend the head pin 45° and loop it around the round-nose pliers. Slide this loop onto the end link of one of the pieces of chain. Hold the loop with the chain-nose pliers and wrap this wire end around to secure. Cut off the excess wire.

13. Repeat step 12 for all four pieces of chain, varying the stones you use each time.

14. Place all four of the completed pieces of chain on the loop that you set aside in step 10. Then hold the loop using the chain-nose pliers and wrap the wire around to secure. Cut off the excess wire.

15. Moving to the closure of the necklace, attach the clasp to three successive strands that you finished in step 8. First, make a new loop in the wire ¾ inch (1.9 cm) from the end. Place the three strands on the loop. Hold the loop with the round-nose pliers and wrap the wires together. Cut off the shorter wire end.

16. Hold the remaining wire with the round-nose pliers and wrap it around again. Slide the clasp onto this loop. Hold the loop with the chain-nose pliers and wrap the wire around the twist you made in step 15.

17. Now make the catch for the clasp. Make a new loop in the 24-gauge wire. Slide onto this loop the remaining three strands. Twist the wires together to secure. Cut off the shorter wire end.

18. Grip the wire using the rubberized round-nose pliers. Loop the wire around. Hold the loop with the rubberized pliers and wrap the wire around the twist you made in step 17 to secure. Cut off the excess wire.

19. To add a final detail for the back of the necklace, make a drop chain, which can also be used as a toggle. First, make a loop in the 24-gauge wire using the round-nose pliers. Run the wire through the smaller loop of the catch for the clasp to attach the loops to each other. Hold this loop with the chain-nose pliers and twist the wires around to secure. Cut off the shorter wire end.

20. Make a new loop using the round-nose pliers. Place the 2-inch (5.1 cm) length of large-link chain onto this loop. Grab the loop with the chain-nose pliers and wrap the wire around the twist you made in step 19. Cut off the excess wire.

21. Select the remaining head pin and slide on your choice of stones. Bend the wire 45°. Loop this wire around the round-nose pliers and place the loop on the end of the chain. Hold the loop with the chain-nose pliers and wrap the wire around to secure. Cut off the excess wire.

reverie

The chunky millefiori glass beads on this necklace evoke Old World charm. Wrapped loops of heavy wire echo the patterns on the ornate bead caps.

Designer: Kate Drew-Wilkinson

Finished size: 25½ inches (64.8 cm) long

Materials

18 silver beads, 2.5 mm

9 lampworked glass beads, 16 mm

3-foot (91.4 cm) length of 18-gauge half-hard sterling silver wire

8-inch (20.3 cm) length of 18-gauge sterling silver chain, 6 x 8 mm

18 silver bead caps, 10 mm

Large heart-shaped silver toggle clasp

Tools

Wire cutters

2 pairs of round-nose pliers

Instructions

1. Cut every third link of the chain to free a pair of links, until you have eight pairs of chain links.

2. Using the wire, make a wrapped bead loop link, attaching one half of the toggle clasp to the loop before closing it. String the link with a silver bead, a bead cap, a glass bead, another bead cap, and a silver bead. Add a pair of chain links to the second loop before you close it. Cut off the remaining wire.

3. Make another wrapped bead loop link, slipping the free chain link from the previous step into the loop before closing it. String the link with beads, as described in step 2, and again add a pair of chain links to the second loop before you close it. Trim the remaining wire. Repeat until you've used all the beads. Add the other half of the toggle clasp to the last loop before closing it.

flapper

Wear this versatile necklace long and open, flapper style; tie one end in a loose overhand knot to make a faux pendant; or double it around your neck for a princess-length contemporary look.

Designer: Nathalie Mornu

Finished Size: 39 inches (99.1 cm)

Materials

7 violet crystals in varying shapes and finishes, 6 to 8 mm

12 violet potato pearls, 7 mm

1 gunmetal split ring, 3.5 mm

1 gunmetal split ring, 5 mm

7 gunmetal split rings, 6 mm

30-inch (76.2 cm) length of gunmetal chain, 1.9 mm

4-foot (1.2 m) length of 26-gauge silver craft wire

Liver of sulfur

Tools

Plastic or glass container for liver of sulfur solution

Wire cutters

Chain-nose pliers

Round-nose pliers

Instructions

1. Drop a pea-size piece of liver of sulfur into a container and dissolve it with a half cup (11.8 cl) of boiling water. *Note:* Liver of sulfur is poisonous; don't handle it with bare hands, and don't employ a container or utensils that have been or will be used in preparing food. Gently form the wire so it fits into the container and place it in the solution until it has a patina that matches the color of the chain. Remove the wire, then rinse and dry it.

2. Cut the chain into 25 pieces of different lengths, none less than ¾ inch (1.9 cm) long. Set aside.

3. Cut a 1½-inch (3.8 cm) piece of wire and make a small wrapped loop at one end, but before you make the wrap, attach the loop to the end link of one of the chain pieces. String one of the beads onto the same wire and make another small wrapped loop at the other end of the wire that attaches to the end of another chain piece (figure 1).

fig. 1

Connect the other end of this chain piece to a split ring. Repeat to create a random strand of beaded links, chain, and split rings. For three of the beaded links use two pearls instead of one (figure 2).

fig. 2

4. Attach the last beaded link to the open end of the first chain piece to close the strand into a necklace.

trade caravan

Simple wire loop and jump ring techniques
create a necklace well worth trading for.

trade caravan

Designer: Karen J. Lauseng

Finished Size: 18 inches (45.7 cm) long

Materials

Strong black tea or coffee

9 bone hairpipe beads, 1 inch (2.5 cm) long

50-inch (127 cm) length of 18-gauge sterling silver round wire

17 random-shaped brass disc beads, 8 mm

9 brass rondelle beads, 8 mm

9 horn rondelle beads, 8 mm

9 skunk Venetian trade beads, 14 mm

21 red-colored African white heart beads, approximately 8 mm

16 brass spacer beads, 4 mm

8 black frosted-glass beads, 10 mm

150 18-gauge sterling jump rings, 3 mm

Clasp

Tools

Cup

Flush cutters

Ruler or tape measure

Fine-tooth flat jeweler's file

Round-nose pliers

2 pairs of chain-nose pliers

Instructions

1. Antique the bone beads by dropping them into a cup of very strong black tea and letting them soak for about a half hour. Check on them often, and remove them when they've reached the desired shade.

2. Use the flush cutters to cut nine 3¼-inch (8.3 cm) lengths of 18-gauge sterling silver wire. File the ends of the wires flat with the jeweler's file.

3. Using your round-nose pliers, form a loop at one end of the wire. Next, add the beads to the wire in the following order:
   • Random-shaped brass disc bead
   • Bone hairpipe bead
   • Brass rondelle
   • Horn rondelle
   • Skunk bead
   • Red-colored white heart bead
   • Brass spacer bead

   When all the beads are in place, use the round-nose pliers to form a loop on the other end of the wire. Repeat this process until you have added beads to all nine sections of the silver wire. This collection of beads will be called Bead Group A (see the process shown in figure 1).

fig. 1

4. Cut eight 1¼-inch (3.2 cm) lengths of 18-gauge sterling silver wire. Prepare the wire as in step 3, and then add the beads in the following order:
    • Brass spacer bead
    • Red-colored white heart bead
    • Brass spacer bead

    Form the closing loop, and repeat the process until you have eight sets. This collection will be called Bead Group B.

    Cut four 1¾-inch (4.4 cm) lengths of 18-gauge sterling silver wire, and prepare the wire in the same manner as in step 3. Add the beads in the following order:
    • Black frosted-glass bead
    • Random-shaped brass disc bead
    • Red-colored white heart bead
    • Random-shaped brass disc bead
    • Black frosted-glass bead

    Form the closing loop, and repeat the process until you have four sets. This collection will be called Bead Group C.

5. Now connect the sections together. Using the two sets of chain-nose pliers, open a jump ring. Slide on one bead set from Group A and one from Group B. Close the jump ring. Use another jump ring to add another Group A set to the other end of the connected Group B set. Continue adding jump rings and bead sets until all of the Group A beads are connected to Group B beads as shown in the main photo.

6. Using jump rings, attach two bead sets from Group C to each end of the chain. Adding an extra jump ring between these bead sets results in more uniform spacing.

7. When all the beads have been connected, continue adding jump rings on both ends of the necklace. The number of jump rings used will vary with the fit. A double chain looks really nice and balances the weight of the beads. Once you are satisfied with the fit, connect the jump rings to a purchased clasp.

Designer's Tip

"White heart beads" are just what their name implies: white at their heart and another color on the outside. The coloring agents used by early bead makers were often relatively expensive, so making trade beads of white glass and only coloring the surface was a more economical choice.

about the designers

Jeannette Chiang Bardi has had a passion for making jewelry ever since she discovered the amazing world of crystals and gemstones. She is inspired by the incredible history of jewelry and has integrated ancient symbolism and techniques into her work. Jeannette is especially fascinated by ancient Egyptian and Chinese jewelry, from the history of wire wrapping to the mystical use of crystals and stones. Visit www.thestonecuttersworkshop.com.

Christine Calla designs jewelry for Half the Sky and is the co-author of Lark Jewelry & Beading's *Beading Vintage-Style Jewelry*. In addition to being an accomplished designer, she is a spa and skincare business owner and the mother of three. She includes her husband in that tally.

Lisa Colby holds a BFA with a concentration in metalsmithing from Wayne State University. She is a self-employed production metalsmith living and working in Asheville, North Carolina. Her work is featured in *1000 Rings*, published by Lark Jewelry & Beading. Among her numerous gallery representations are Bellagio Gallery, Asheville, North Carolina; Penland Gallery at Penland School of Crafts, Penland, North Carolina; and the Signature Shop and Gallery in Atlanta, Georgia.

Patty Cox developed nearly half of the projects in *Dazzling Bead & Wire Crafts*. Her 25 designs for that book included jewelry, napkin rings, a picture frame, cocktail skewers, a clock, and a bookmark.

Cynthia Deis has been making tiny things since childhood, when she took apart garage-sale jewelry to create new trinkets for her dolls. She worked as a teacher and a window dresser before selling her jewelry professionally under the trade name Bedizen Ornaments. She lives in Raleigh, North Carolina, where she writes a mixed-media craft blog, teaches, and works in her bead store. Her website is www.ornamentea.com.

Molly Dingledine is a studio jeweler working in Asheville, North Carolina. She graduated in 2005 from the Savannah College of Art and Design with a BFA in metals and jewelry. She is represented in many galleries and sells her work at fine craft shows. Fascinated with the forms and textures of nature, Molly has always found inspiration in the natural world, whether hiking mountain trails or strolling down city streets. She builds on the simple shapes found in nature to create complex art forms. Her work can be seen at www.mollydingledine.com.

Kate Drew-Wilkinson was born and raised in England and began her professional life as an actress. She was always fascinated by the history and magic of beads, however, and during her travels in many countries, she studied their use in jewelry. By 1990, Kate had discovered the joy of lampworking. She has written two books on bead jewelry and 48 articles for *Lapidary Journal Jewelry Artist*, and she also makes instructional films. Kate teaches bead jewelry design and lampworked bead making in Europe. Go to http://katedrew-wilkinson.com/wordpress/.

Kathy Frey is an artist in all aspects of her life. She enjoys cooking, gardening, and home decorating projects. In 2009, she moved to a small artists' community in rural Northern California so she could commune with nature on a regular basis. Her pursuits are expressed creatively in her sculptural wire jewelry designs, which are abstract expressions of the pleasures she finds in simplicity, she says. You can learn more about Kathy via her website, www.kathyfrey.com, where there's also a link to her "Taming the Tangle" blog.

Ellen Gerritse has traveled extensively and taught fine arts in Europe and Asia. She creates objects from accessible materials with a few tools she has at hand. She won the Collectors' Choice Award during the Mind Over Metal show in Houston, Texas. Ellen owns and operates Gerritse, a gallery in Middelburg, Netherlands. Find Ellen's work at www.ellengerritse.kunstinzicht.nl.

Elizabeth Glass Geltman and **Rachel Geltman** are the mother-daughter design team behind www.geltdesigns.com. Their work has been published in the Lark Jewelry & Beading books *500 Earrings* and *New Directions in Metal Clay*, as well as numerous other publications.

Joanna Gollberg is a studio jeweler in Asheville, North Carolina. In addition to making jewelry, she is the author of four Lark Jewelry & Beading books: *Making Metal Jewelry*, *Creative Metal Crafts*, *The Art & Craft of Making Jewelry*, and *The Ultimate Jeweler's Guide*. Joanna teaches jewelry making at craft schools, including Penland School of Crafts and Arrowmont School of Arts and Crafts, as well as for metalsmithing groups across the country. She exhibits her work at fine craft shows and galleries nationally. See more at www.joannagollberg.com.

Ndidi Kowalczyk is a fashion and surface design artist with degrees from Drexel University and the Philadelphia College of Textiles and Science. Ndidi was drawn to jewelry design because it is portable, with instant gratification. She combines her loves of movement, color, and texture to create one-of-a-kind accessories.

Nancy Kugel was born and raised in St. Louis, Missouri, and has always had an interest in fine crafts, including needlework, basketry, and metalwork. She discovered her love of beading years ago, and finds inspiration everywhere she travels.

Mami Laher is a jewelry designer and artist who loves, more than anything, searching for originality and uniqueness in creative expression. She prides herself on making bead and wire jewelry with no jig, only basic tools. She enjoys painting with watercolors and has an affinity for flowers, abstract as well as real. She can also be found ice skating.

Mami originally hails from Japan but now resides in Los Angeles. View a sampling of her jewelry, glass beads, and paintings at www.mamibeads.com.

Elizabeth Larsen works as a biologist for Snohomish County in Washington. She started beading as a hobby in 2001. Her work has been published in beading magazines and books and can be seen on her blog http://saichandesigns.blogspot.com.

Linda Larsen started a love affair with color and texture many years ago. She explored a range of arts and crafts until she encountered jewelry design and metalwork and was smitten. She owns www.objectsandelements.com, where she gets to play out all her design ideas.

Janet A. Lasher has been creating embellished textiles, beadwork, and other wearable art forms since she was old enough to sit in front of a sewing machine. In 2004, she left her corporate position in order to focus on developing more complicated fiber sculptures. Her work is found in private and corporate collections, including the Bernina International Collection in Switzerland. Janet works in her studio, teaches embellishment and surface design, and lives with her husband and son in Charlotte, North Carolina. Find out more about Janet's work at www.janetalasher.com.

Karen J. Lauseng is a New Mexico artist whose artwork has appeared in numerous publications. She has displayed her pieces in more than 100 venues, including solo exhibitions, juried shows, and galleries. See for yourself at www.kjartworks.net.

Sandra Lupo teaches jewelry making and metalsmithing at the Newark Museum Arts Workshop and at nearby bead shops in New Jersey. She also teaches at regional and national events. Her designs have appeared in several books. Sandra is a member of the team of experts for Fire Mountain Gems and Beads Ask the Experts, and she is a Swarovski Elements Ambassador. Visit www.sandsstones.com.

Valérie MacCarthy makes jewelry that combines the beauty of nature and the inspiring simplicity of colors and shapes. She got her start in jewelry when her grandmother gave her a box of beads and some string at age 7. An opera singer by trade, Valérie authored the Lark Jewelry & Beading book *Beading with Gemstones*. Find out more about Valérie at www.valeriemaccarthy.com.

Andrea L. McLester had the pleasure of creating jewelry for some of the world's legendary ballerinas and opera singers during her costuming career. She now resides in Salado, Texas, where she helped found the Salado Arts Workshop, a nonprofit arts education organization dedicated to providing professional artist training that serves as a springboard for emerging artists. She is working to promote sustainable art by producing a series of jewelry pieces, bowls, platters, and sculptures made exclusively from recycled glass. Find out more about her and her designs at www.andreamclester.com.

Kaari Meng is the owner and operator of the Hollywood-based store French General. She teaches jewelry making and creates and sells vintage beading kits and home décor accessories. She has designed jewelry for companies such as Anthropologie and has sold her jewelry to specialty shops around the world. She is the author of the Lark Jewelry & Beading title *French-Inspired Jewelry* and has been featured in the magazines *O, Martha Stewart Living*, and *Romantic Homes*. Discover Kaari and her work at www.frenchgeneral.com.

Chris Franchetti Michaels is the author of several popular craft books, including the bestseller *Teach Yourself Visually: Jewelry Making & Beading*. You can learn more about her work on her website, www.beadjewelry.net.

Nathalie Mornu is an editor for the Lark Jewelry & Beading team. She has dabbled in many crafts over the years, so as a sideline she sometimes creates projects for Lark publications—stuff as varied as stitched potholders, a weird scarecrow made from cutlery, and a gingerbread igloo. Her author credits include *Chains Chains Chains*, the bestselling *A Is for Apron*, and *Leather Jewelry*.

Brenda Schweder is a nationally recognized jeweler and teacher and the author of three books: *Steel Wire Jewelry*, *Junk to Jewelry*, and *Vintage Redux*. Brenda's designs and fashion jewelry forecasts have been published more than 100 times in books and magazines. Visit her at www.brendaschweder.com.

Andrea L. Stern grew up surrounded by artists, so she knew one day she'd make some kind of art. She started with drawings and then moved on to painting, beadwork, and quilting. You can find samples of her work at http://andreasternart.blogspot.com and www.embellishmentcafe.com.

Marty Stevens-Heebner is the president and creator of the Rebagz Handbags line. The company was named 2009 California Small Business of the Year, and Marty was named one of the "Top 20 Inspiring Women of 2010" by *CocoEco Magazine*. Marty is also an author and has been called a "fashion outlaw" because of the chances she takes in her designs, her life, and her way of doing business.

Christine Strube started working with beads when she began employment at Sorella Beads, a bead store and lampworking studio in St. Louis, Missouri. She met and was inspired by many talented bead artists, including Stephanie Sersich, Dustin Tabor, Kate McKinnon, and Cindy Jenkins. Since then, she has begun teaching her own classes, selling jewelry at juried shows, and publishing projects in magazines such as *Bead&Button*, *Step by Step Beads*, and *Beadwork*.

index

project index

This list will help you find projects made using specific types of beads or techniques; you'll find it helpful if you already know the primary kinds of materials or processes you want to use to make your necklaces.

acknowledgments

Deepest thanks to Dawn Dillingham, Abby Haffelt, and Hannah Doyle, who did the bulk of the editorial work on this book. Art director Carol Morse Barnao finessed the layouts. I appreciate art intern Jessica Yee's diligence and swiftness. But most importantly, without the project designers who shared their talents in this book, this book wouldn't exist—and necks across the world wouldn't look quite as pretty.